IN OLD
PUNTA GORDA

With
Angie Larkin

Library of Congress Control Number 2001131173
ISBN: 0-9707681-0-9
Book design and production: Tabby House
Cover design: OspreyDesign
Illustrations: Rodman E. Tabor, M.D.
Revised edition
The book evolved from a series of newspaper articles written by Angie Larkin for the city of Punta Gorda's centennial in 1987. Among the revisions, editors for the second edition have updated details, eliminated some redundancies and added illustrations.

This book is dedicated to the man with the velvet whip,
my husband, Kenneth B. Larkin, my cheering section, the thorn in
my side the burr under my saddle . . . for his never-ceasing
encouragement and always constructive criticism,
for his generosity of time, patience,
tenacious faith and careful editing,
his daily urging and constant prodding, which
left me no recourse but to
WRITE!
WRITE!
WRITE!

Old Punta Gorda, Inc.
P.O. Box 510595
Punta Gorda, FL 33950

List of Sponsors

In Memory of Ken Larkin
Paul and Elizabeth Ditto
Garnett Scholl
U.S. Cleveland
John and Fran Campbell
Norma and Fred Powers
W. Wayne and Deborah Woodard
Madeleine and J. Peter Schmid
Keep up the good work, Old Punta Gorda—Art and Edna Butler
To know our past helps guide our future
Florida Adventure Museum
Max J. Cleveland
Don and Pak Atwell
In memory of William D. Johnson
Thankful for our cottage in Old P.G., Brian and Deb Strauch
Remember those who came before
In memory of Albert A. Quednau
Ken and Kay Sanders
For Lillian, a loyal fan, Angie
We know her as "Mimi," and she told us (three sons) while grown up
        that she would someday do this. Congratulations, Mimi!
In support of a wonderful community.
Make history. Bloom where you are planted.
Gertrude Haage
Stephen, Jake, and Lindsey Kaznak
In memory of Mayor Bill Richards

In honor of Whit James Jones, born September 15, 1901 on Cabbage
    Key, Punta Gorda
In memory of Alberta Curry Jones, a descendant of
    William A. Williams, a certified Florida pioneer
Here's to memories and history
Carol Mahler
Claire Ann Miller
Rachel Rebekah Renne
Aubrey Leigh Leonard
Jahna Peace Leonard
Remembering old friends/Audrey Muccio
In memory of J. Clarke Cassidy, Jr.
Punta Gorda—our lovely hometown
Grayce Johnson Myers—born on A. C. Frizzell's ranch, 1928
Pamella Seay and Perry and Audre Seay
Bob Parker

Partially funded by a grant from the Arts and Humanities Council of
Charlotte County Inc.

Acknowledgments

This book would not have been possible without the encouragement and friendliness of scores of native-born Punta Gordans and long-term residents of the Charlotte Harbor area. The names of these new friends are found throughout these pages. Thank you, all. — *Angie Larkin*

Old Punta Gorda, Inc., gratefully acknowledges the donation of time and talent by Rodman E. Tabor, M.D., to produce the sketches used to illustrate this edition of *In Old Punta Gorda.*

Dr. Tabor used background material from the following two books by Lindsey Williams and U. S. Cleveland as additional inspiration for his drawings: *Our Fascinating Past; Charlotte Harbor: The Early Years*, and *Our Fascinating Past; Charlotte Harbor: The Later Years.*

Preface

If you've picked up this book expecting to peruse a historical tome, put it right back on the shelf. *In Old Punta Gorda* is a loving visit with the people who lived "way back then." The writer is a newcomer to Punta Gorda who has long since adopted it as her own hometown. Here are fishermen, lawyers, schoolteachers and mechanics, housewives and cowboys, grocers and doctors. They all have one thing in common: they are natives or very long-term residents with strong feelings of love and affection for their town the way it used to be.

Memories are often ephemeral, like half-remembered dreams and, as such, may change with each individual recollection. Because of this, there may be some discrepancies in these tales. This is, after all, not a history book and should not be read as such.

The people in these pages have welcomed me into their homes, laughed and sometimes cried with me. They have confided in me (some with tales I could never put into print), shared their past in a way that has brightened and brought to life faded photographs of old Punta Gorda.

Today when I walk into Publix market, I am stepping onto the spacious verandah of the Hotel Punta Gorda with its climbing roses and welcoming front entrance. When I drive out Marion Avenue, I'm riding behind a herd of cattle driven by sweating cowboys in those strange old hats as they push the critters toward the cattle-loading dock at the west end of town. When I cross the Peace River bridge I see Miss Esther McCullough hopping daintily onto the mail boat on her way to teach school in Charlotte Harbor across the bay.

At the post office, in a last minute rush to mail cards to friends in faraway places, I take a moment to look across the street at the old

Arcade, picturing it in its days of glory, bustling with last minute shoppers taking time to sip a cherry smash in Maxwell's Drug Store while waiting for the mail train.

This then is the story of Trabue/Punta Gorda; its birth, its struggles, its heyday and its growth to the small city it is today. Its pioneer families, its loving citizens, have told this story. They are truly a breed apart. This story is written for them.

Indeed, this book was written by them.

Contents

The Town of Trabue

The Indians were here first, the fierce Calusas and, later, the Seminoles. More than 400 years ago Cuban fishermen sailed by the lush peninsula they called Punta Gorda, "fat point." In 1513 and again in 1521, the Spaniards came exploring under the leadership of Juan Ponce de Leon. Ponce was fatally wounded by a Calusa arrow and his men set sail for Cuba where he died.

There was quiet amid the mangroves and palmettos for a long time; then came the Seminole Wars in the mid 1800s and that proud tribe was forced south into the Everglades to make room for the white man. With the departure of the Indians, early frontiersmen appeared on the scene. One of the pioneers was James Madison Lanier, a hardy hunter and trapper from Fort Ogden.

He settled in a small cabin on the south shore of the Peace River about where the old banyan tree on Retta Esplanade now stands. An earlier settlement, Hickory Bluff (Charlotte Harbor) had been started across the bay by an influx of fishermen from Harkers Island, North Carolina. Lanier traded with them and with the Seminoles, who paddled their canoes around the point.

In 1880, a Chicago newspaperman wrote about the lush beauty of this virgin land. Colonel Isaac Trabue of Louisville, Kentucky, and a Civil War veteran, read the article and that same year arrived upon the scene. He was enthralled with the tropical surroundings and immediately purchased approximately thirty acres from Lanier. The farsighted colonel started a settlement on the site, hiring Captain Kelly B. Harvey to survey and plat the new village, which the colonel named modestly Trabue.

Years later in 1924, answering a surveying query from Colonel Hancock, attorney for the city of Punta Gorda, this same Kelly B. Harvey describes vividly this section of Florida before the turn of the century.

"Tampa was only a mere village and Southwest Florida a wilderness without rail transportation south of Jacksonville. The only buildings on the map south of Bartow were a Spanish palmetto shack for salting fish on Captiva, one at Gasparilla, post offices at Fort Myers, Punta Rassa, Charlotte Harbor, Fort Ogden, Pine Level, Joshua Creek and Fort Meade. There was a store at each place with a handful of goods. Mail was received twice a month and bacon, coffee and brogan shoes arrived once a month from Cedar Key on Captain Hodson's sailing ship *Mallory,* which would return with deer hides and oranges from scattered settlements of log cabins throughout the woods."

As a surveyor-engineer for the Disston Land Company, he described his job. "Alone for months, banqueting on grits and bacon, sugarless coffee; sleeping the sweetest of dreams, feet to a campfire, a saddle for a pillow, two rainproof wool blankets and mother earth for a couch, downpouring rain or a starry sky above, I'd be lulled to sleep by the murmuring pines, the chattering birds and the racket of wild animal life—guarded over by my faithful Florida pony. One morning I found I had made my bed by a large rattlesnake, which had found shelter with me by a palmetto clump, from a chilling northwestern gale. The rattler was too cold to put up an argument with his bedfellow."

Harvey further writes that Punta Gorda was overrun with bums, gamblers, toughs and adventurers. There were five murders in the year 1886 alone. The only jail was a boxcar; there were no streets, sidewalks or ditches. The swampland nurtured palmetto and pine brush, and also bred fierce mosquitoes. "When it rained, we waded, and the few lady pioneers stayed home."

Colonel Trabue, the largest property owner, could not be induced to contribute any drainage works or public improvements. This total lack of consideration on his part led the townsfolk to a secret, but legal, meeting and little Trabue was officially incorporated under the new name of Punta Gorda on December 7, 1887, and the town of Trabue was no more, but the colonel had left a legacy—the railroad.

Railroad and Fishing

With the advent of the railroad, this little town blossomed. The railroad brought in Georgia pine and myriad materials to build the hotel. It brought in carloads of workers, carpenters, masons and plumbers from the North and, eventually the necessary help to maintain such a large establishment. But most of all was the tremendous boost the railroad gave the fishing industry. Punta Gorda had started out primarily as a cattle and fishing village, but it was one thing to ship cattle by boat to Cuba and quite another to transport fish outside the area. The cattle were on the hoof. To ship fresh fish long distances by boat was not possible without spoilage.

1886 train arriving in Punta Gorda.
Sketch by R. Tabor.

Workers now built a 400-foot-long pier out into the harbor capable of supporting a loaded railroad train. Next, a narrow-gauge railway was erected to run from the ice house on King Street and Virginia to the fish houses at the end of the pier. A donkey engine hauled the ice down and the fish were then packed in ice and loaded onto the waiting freight cars. Fishing had now become a full-scale industry. Woodrow Goff remembers seeing refrigerated cars loaded to the gills with fish, as many as seven carloads in one day—5,000 pounds of fish to the carload! Charlotte Harbor's vast supply of fish could now be carried away by rail.

Hotel Punta Gorda

The building of the resort hotel accelerated and the result was a vast, sprawling wooden structure complete with tower for viewing the busy river traffic. A verandah surrounded the building and trellises were covered with climbing roses. It was a spectacular sight and could be seen for miles. The hotel tower was always well lighted at night and boats on the bay used it as a beacon.

The Hotel Punta Gorda brought new business and prosperity to the town. Generally the hotel guests stayed aloof from the local gentry as though there were an invisible wall between them.

However, local brass bands did play for the guests as they strolled the beautiful grounds—the ladies resplendent in their Paris gowns and twirling lacy parasols to protect them from the hot sun. The clientele was mainly the wealthy and renowned. Names such as Theodore Roosevelt, Winston Churchill and Andrew Mellon appeared on the guest register.

The Mysterious Mr. McAdow

Around the turn of the century, when the Hotel Punta Gorda was at the peak of its popularity, the evening train pulled in discharging, among others, a man in a wheelchair. Several guests, rocking on the hotel verandah, enjoying the colorful sunset, commented on this. In spite of the wheelchair and his obvious disability, he seemed to command respect. Who was he?

Perry W. McAdow, an extremely wealthy and influential man, had decided to make Punta Gorda his home. Enthralled by the harbor view and undaunted by the late Trabue's designation of all waterfront property as park lands, he prevailed upon the city fathers to let him build a home where the Best Western now stands. He managed this by promising that, after his death and that of his wife, the property would revert to the city.

He further promised to "dress it up like a park," and that he did, planting all sorts of exotic plants and flowers on the property, including a banyan tree.

The great home he built was a huge, frame structure of three stories, painted white, with a sprawling porch that encircled it. It became a dazzling landmark on the harbor front along with the big hotel. His wife, Marian, was a lover of the arts and of the nicer things in life. The spacious rooms overlooking the harbor were filled with handsome furnishings and the walls with glowing paintings. There were oriental rugs throughout, even on the porch and Mrs. McAdow decorated the banisters with colorful scarves and hangings; there were Japanese lanterns ringing the verandah. It certainly was an unusual home for this little town.

There was always a bit of mystery about the McAdows. Perry was a very private person, not prone to talk about himself and no one was absolutely sure where he came from and what accident had confined him to a wheelchair. Some said he owned a large mine "out west" and that it was there he met with the accident that broke his spine and incapacitated his legs. Whatever had happened in the past, Perry could not walk and had to be lifted in and out of his wheelchair. A ramp was built from the porch so he could wheel himself (or be pushed) to a boat shed at the dock and onto his boat, the *Roamer*.

Perry McAdow lived in this fashion in our town for thirty years, dying at the age of eighty-three in 1918. His funeral was as unique as the rest of his life here. He had planned, years before, to be cremated—something that wasn't common in those days. He had wanted to have his body placed on the *Roamer* and the boat set afire out in the harbor—shades of the old Vikings. Friends had talked him out of this by reminding him the boat would burn only to the waterline and remain a

Perry McAdow in his wheelchair under the banyan tree. Sketch by R. Tabor

navigational hazard in the harbor. So Perry selected a remote area outside of town and, pledging to secrecy the farmer who owned the property, had the man erect a pyre of lightwood knots to Perry's specifications.

On a steaming sultry night, young Henry Farrington was told by his uncle, Albert Dewey, to "get the car ready to pick up Mrs. McAdow, we're going to cremate Mr. McAdow." Young Henry, stunned almost speechless, did as he was told, picked up Mrs. McAdow and a lady friend and drove to where the hearse, a doctor and undertaker were waiting.

Another uncle of Henry's had a Model T that had been cut down to a small truck and Perry's casket was loaded onto that. The small convoy of automobile and truck started the trek to the farmer's home; not even Mrs. McAdow knew the location of the funeral pyre. The farmer, lantern in hand, led the small procession to the designated spot. The casket was placed onto the six-foot-high pile of pine logs; gallons of kerosene were poured on the wood, "someone lit it and it went up with a big woosh—just like that. We stayed out there until dawn and when we left there was just a great bed of coals there."

The next afternoon Mrs. McAdow asked Henry to take a galvanized tub and shovel and bring back Perry McAdow's ashes. Perry had stipulated he wanted them strewn around his favorite jacaranda tree. The young boy returned to the scene, finding nothing left but ashes and the metal handles of the casket. Using the coffin handles as markers, he retrieved some mortal remains of Mr. McAdow; the ashes were placed where Perry McAdow willed them. Old Punta Gorda remembers to this day the funeral pyre of Mr. Perry McAdow.

Teddy Pays a Call

Theodore Roosevelt, twenty-sixth president of our country, was the most celebrated fisherman in Punta Gorda, having caught one of the largest monster devilfish in the world in this area.

Thereby hangs a tale. Young Belle McBean (Quednau), heard that the president was going out fishing on Captain McCann's boat and, hoping to catch a glimpse of the famous toothy grin, she rode her bike down to the dock. Sure enough she heard the well-known booming voice ring out loud and clear. "We haven't got a Kodak! Who in blazes forgot the camera?" "I've got one. I've got one" piped up our Belle. "I'll go get it."

Off she went, her young legs pumping up a breeze as she raced home to get her treasured Brownie. Flushed with pride (and perspiration) she handed over her little camera to the president. Later, Belle's camera was returned with many thanks and Teddy Roosevelt left for the White House. In a few weeks a beautiful new camera, complete with tripod, arrived at the McBean home—a present from the big man himself.

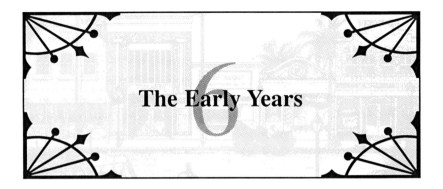

The 6 Early Years

The town was growing up; stores began to spring up along Marion Avenue, professional men appeared on the scene and banks were established. Byron Rhode, who grew up here, says, "I can pretty well put things together as far back as 1909." He remembers when the woods around Punta Gorda, north, south, east and west were virgin pine forests; the trees had not even been turpentined. As for businesses, he remembers one in particular. "H. W. Smith had a bakery, no bigger than a two-car garage; he used to bake the bread, put it on a little wagon and peddle it up and down the street. Other merchants would buy his bakery goods, put them in a glass case, unwrapped and unsliced. That little bakery grew into a business that covered the whole street." He eventually owned a whole block on Marion with a bakery, market, restaurant and the Bay View Hotel. He also remembers a livery stable on Herald Court next to the first jail. Jim Goff ran it and there was another one near the courthouse.

Byron Rhode had been born up north, in Williston, Florida, in 1904 and had moved to Punta Gorda when he was "a little tot." His family home is still standing on Sullivan Street and he remembers when "the town was just a little village. At the intersection of Cross and Marion there was an artesian well with a pipe fountain and a tin cup attached for the thirsty passerby, and a trough for horses and oxen. The city hall was a small one-story block building with a shed on the side. In this shed was stored a two-wheeled fire cart with a long tongue. When there was a fire, the icehouse would blow its whistle and the townspeople would race to the shed, grab the tongue of the cart and pull it to the blaze."

There was no sewage system and there were outhouses in the alleys back of the homes. An old black man, Alex Stephens, drove a white mule hitched to a two-wheel cart up and down these alleys and cleaned out the privies for fifty cents a month. There were no bridges across the river, only two or three autos in town and no paved roads to run them on. When night descended on the town, a few kerosene street lamps mounted on poles were lit by hand and at dawn they were extinguished. The streets were unpaved and the sidewalks were wooden boards.

Byron Rhode remembers the funeral pyre of eccentric and wealthy Perry McAdow. He recalls Miss Norma Pepper's private school on Olympia Avenue and King Street (northbound U.S 41) when it was a dusty railroad siding and the station was located across U.S. 41 approximately a block south of the Barron Collier bridge.

I first met Byron Rhode a few years back. He had journeyed down from his home in Jacksonville to attend a family reunion. His visit to his hometown had evoked memories and a sadness in the man. He said, "Walking through the streets, I didn't see a soul I knew. But when I visited Indian Springs cemetery there were all my friends. I recognized name after name, family after family. I stood and looked out over gravestones of families side by side. Finally I sat down under a tree by the creek and thought—here are my friends, here is the Punta Gorda I used to know."

This past spring, on Old Timers' Day, I ran into Byron Rhode again, this time surrounded by old neighbors and friends on the steps of city hall, watching the parade go by. He seemed a happy man, contentedly enjoying the town today but he must have been remembering when the latchstring was always out in the homes of Punta Gorda, when everybody knew everybody and when Belle Quednau was "the prettiest girl in town."

The Quednau Family

Belle Quednau was born in 1891 in Sumter, South Carolina, the daughter of Ludovic McBean, an energetic Scotsman who came to this country from Glasgow in the mid-'80s. He became an officer in the Salvation Army, courted and married a lovely young lady who was to become Belle's mother.

The family remained in Sumter until a frightening malaria epidemic swept the town. Two of Belle's brothers died of the disease and Ludovic decided to move his little family further south to Florida.

Boarding the train and saying farewell to Sumter, the McBeans set out for Fort Myers where Ludovic had been promised a job with H. E. Heitman, owner of vast orange groves. He became engineer on a boat bringing the fruit from Estero to Fort Myers where it was loaded on a train. The family lived on Estero for two years while the head of the house plied the waters back and forth with the valuable cargo. They were happy in their new surroundings until Ludovic was seriously injured when a heavy crate of oranges fell on him and he was no longer able to do any type of hard labor.

Ludovic went to work for the Punta Gorda Fish Company, managing one of its ice houses in Carlos. After a short time he was promoted to another position for the same company in Punta Gorda and moved his family here. They lived on Goldstein Street right across the street from where Belle lives today. The first school in Punta Gorda was next door, so Belle never had an excuse to be tardy!

Belle remembers her first Christmas in Punta Gorda. She and her five siblings hopped out of bed at sunup to see what Santa had brought. Their Christmas stockings were filled with homemade candy, apples and nuts. "I'll never forget my favorite toy—probably still somewhere in the attic. It was a Chinese doll in a lovely kimono. Mama had started cooking weeks before Christmas, fruitcake, barbecued pork, ham. She put everything in a big lard can, sealed it tight and set it down our well. The pies and cakes she would bake later as they wouldn't keep. Dinner was in the middle of the day because we had only kerosene lamps, not fit for a holiday dinner. Chicken and dumplings, ham and barbecued pork, sweet potato pie and for desert, mincemeat pie, lemon pie and fruitcake!" A tired but happy little girl tumbled into bed that night.

Belle went to school right next door and remembers that the roads in town were mainly dirt with the exception of a few that were paved with oyster shells. She and her friends used to swim down at the bay; "Mrs. McAdow let us swim in front of her house where there were steps going down into the water. About half of us didn't have bathing suits; we'd swim in our old clothes. We used to go crabbing a lot, take a big tub and a crab net out to where the Isles is now.

"There was one picture show, no talking or anything like that, and it cost a dime." Harry Goldstein, who owned the picture house, provided musical background for the silent movies; he played the violin. A friend of Belle's played the cornet and someone else, the piano—a lot of entertainment for a dime! After the show, there was Mobley's Seminole Pharmacy for a big soda (a dime) or a nickel ice cream cone.

When Belle was a very young girl living on Estero, she had met a handsome young boy who at seventeen was the youngest captain to sail this coast. It was truly love at first sight but Fred Quednau had to wait for Belle to grow up. In the meantime she moved to Punta Gorda, attended school and enjoyed her girlhood.

She left school in the eighth grade to work in the local packing house, crating oranges, grapefruit and tangerines for the grove owners. Ludovic's health was failing and Belle was fast becoming an important breadwinner in the family. The fruit shipping business was a lucrative one, especially during the height of the season. Six girls worked in the packing house and, according to Belle, they made more money than the teachers.

There was a talented seamstress in town, Miss Rhoda Adams, who did all the sewing for the rich guests at the hotel. She taught young

Belle all the intricacies of her handicraft and soon Belle was packing fruit in the winter and sewing in the summertime for a much-needed income.

Belle was working in the packing house when the 1918 Armistice was signed and she'll never forget that day. "We were all working away when the train came down King Street, its whistle blowing to beat the band, flags were waving, horns tooting and people were dancing in the street. That was a day!"

The courtship of Belle McBean and youthful Cap'n Fred Quednau was a prolonged one. Both young people, though much in love, had strong family obligations. Belle's father had never really recovered from his injury on Estero and there were six children in the family; Belle was an important contributor to the family income. "Fred's daddy had died when he was four years old and he and his brothers had to go to work early in life to help their mother support the family."

Fritz Quednau arrived in Punta Gorda from Germany in the late 1800s and opened the first cigar factory on Marion Avenue. He and his wife had three sons, one of whom was Fred, born in 1892. When Fred was only four years old, his father died and life became a struggle for the youngster and his brothers. Mrs. Quednau had to go out and work to feed her children; among the people she worked for were Mrs. Trabue and Mrs. McAdow. Fred and his brothers left school at an early age and went to work on the run boats. After a long day's work, the boys were taught at night by the legendary Norma Pepper. As a captain, Fred, was in the position to ask for his true love's hand.

Belle and Fred Quednau were the second couple to be married in Charlotte County after its break from DeSoto County, the first being Austin and Bertha Powell.

Cap'n Fred Stays Ashore

Cap'n Fred loaded cargo in Punta Gorda, essential items for the people living further south: flour, sugar, yard goods, lumber, tools, dynamite and even "white lightning." Belle traveled on the boat with him; there was a stateroom for the captain, a cook on board and a crew of eight, so Belle traveled in comfort. She enjoyed these trips, doing her sewing and crocheting while drinking in the beautiful scenery. Even when their daughter, Tosie (Hindman), was born, Belle still sailed with Cap'n Fred and the little girl became a natural sailor.

As Tosie approached school age, there had to be a drastic change in the Quednau lifestyle. Belle became a landlubber again while Tosie started her education. Cap'n Fred endured this separation from his little family for a while and then gave up his sailing days for good. He had always enjoyed cooking and decided to try to make a living at it. In 1929 he opened Fred's Quick Lunch on Marion Avenue (Where Waldo's Bistro is now) and ran it successfully for seventeen years. Always a gregarious and friendly man, he entered city politics, first as a council-man, then becoming mayor in the '30s and going on to be sheriff of Charlotte County. The marriage of the little girl from Estero and Punta Gorda and the young lad working the boats was a long and happy one. Belle is now a widow lady still living on Goldstein Street across from her old schoolhouse (now an apartment building) and content with her memories of Cap'n Fred and their life together. Her daughter, Tosie Hindman, county supervisor of election for many years, lives not far away and tries to keep an eye on her very active mother.

Cattle Drives

The cattle industry was an integral part of Florida's early growth. Gladys Wilt's great-grandfather was Jesse Knight who, in the 1820s was one of the pioneer cattlemen in the state. His place, Knight's Station, is still on the map east of Tampa. At the height of Knight's cattle "empire," his holdings stretched east to the Myakka River and south almost to Charlotte Harbor where 20,000 head of cattle grazed.

A generation later, sometime before the Civil War, Gladys' grandfather, Shadrick "Shade" Hancock, also headed south with his cattle from Georgia to a new life in Florida. On the long journey from Georgia Shade stopped off at Knight's Station, worked for a while for Jesse, long enough to fall in love with Sara Jane, one of Jesse's fifteen children.

After a festive wedding at Knight's Station, Shade and Sara started off on Shade's original trek to the rich flat lands on the upper Myakka River. The settlement was called Myakka, and Shade drove his cattle from there down along a trail blazed by an earlier cattleman named King (Kings Highway) to big pens on the north side of Peace River. The land was high there, the water deep and the Charlotte Harbor dock was an ideal spot from which to load the cattle onto waiting Spanish ships bound for Cuba and South America.

Shade was always paid in Spanish gold which he placed in his saddlebag and guarded carefully on the long ride back to Myakka. Once home, he would toss the bag over in a corner of the barn until he had time to count it and carry it to the nearest bank some distance off in Bradentown as it was then called. Shade was a highly religious man, a lay preacher who proceeded to build three churches in the area within two years. One was in Pine Level and another in Myakka; the latter has been preserved and still stands in the town. He also built a school house for the itinerant teachers who traveled the countryside.

In the Punta Gorda area, shipments of beeves were at their highest between 1901 and 1908. Cattle were driven out Marion Avenue to a loading dock west of town and herded onto boats sailing to Cuba. Roundup time was one of excitement and noise in town. The cattle that had been roaming the vast open range, were used to their freedom and rebelled against the pushing drovers. The cowboys, on the other hand, found the herding job a thirsty and sweltering one, their arrival in town after weeks on the range was exhilarating to the extent that many riders ended the day in the town calaboose after one too many for the road.

In 1908 Cuba imposed an import tax on cattle, about $2.50 per head on common cattle and shipments gradually ceased with concentration now on domestic sales. Outstanding cattlemen, legends unto themselves were: the King brothers, J. W. Whidden, R. E. Whidden, T. S. Knight and Frank Knight. Following these earlier cattlemen were A. C. Frizzell and W. Luther Koon.

Snake Whidden

James Edward Whidden Sr. was born in 1904 in a frame house in Charlotte Harbor just northeast of where Rolls Landing is now. His father, Robert J. Whidden, had cattle of his own but was also W. Luther Koon's ranch foreman and rode the range making a living for his two children, James Edward and Florence. The little boy and his sister trudged through the fields to school carrying their lunch. During recess they played games with names like Dare Base, Pop the Whip and Prison Base. James said he was "nicknamed 'Snake' 'cause I was so silly."

After school, Snake's job was to see that all the calves were in the cow pen awaiting their mothers' daily visit. Every cow has her own special spot of grazing land, her own home on the range. She would come to the pen to tend to her offspring, to be milked and then returned to pasture.

Snake's first home burned to the ground about 1906 when he was too young to remember it. He does remember the second fire. His dad had rebuilt, this time a two-story house on higher ground. One day Snake, his sister and their father were away from home working a sweet potato patch in a distant field. "Suddenly, looking homeward, Dad saw smoke, ripped the harness off the horse, loosened him from the plow, jumped on him bareback and took off for home." Unfortunately it was too late to save the house. Some men had been clearing brush (under his father's orders), burning palmetto growth around the homestead and a live ash must have blown through an open window. "We were the only ones living out there and there was no such thing as a fire department. There was nothing we could do about it." Nothing daunted, his father cleared the land and built a third home on the same site.

When Snake was eight years old, his dad gave him ten head of cattle and the boy herded them on one of his father's horses, a white mare that was blind in one eye. She was a woods horse, one that knew how to herd cattle. When he was nine, Snake went to work on his first cattle drive. "I weighed forty pounds soaking wet. Dad was delivering a bunch of steers to Tampa and we were seven days on the road driving cattle, three of us and a big old shepherd dog. I rode Dad's white mare and my saddle was a McClellan, an old cavalry favorite. On the return trip my dad carried me to the zoo in Sulfur Springs for the first half a day and then we spent the other two and a half days riding home."

Snake remembers how long that trip was. He also recalls how long it took to go from his home in Charlotte Harbor to Punta Gorda—nine hours! There was no bridge across the river and he and his dad had to ride their horses by way of Fort Ogden. However, Snake enjoyed these trips, in fact he enjoyed everything that took him away from school. When he was sixteen, the law said he could quit school and that he did. "I put my hat on my head and went whistling down the road.

"First thing I did when I left school was to go down in the bay— fishing for John Strickland." This job lasted for about three months when Snake found out that, not only was he not making money, he was $2.50 in the hole! Then he hit the cow trail, driving cattle for the Hollingsworth Brothers out of Arcadia. His first drive with this outfit was an unnerving experience.

"There were two separate herds of cattle: older steers (more than two years old) in a herd driven by one group of cowboys and the two-year-olds in another—that was the one I was in. At night when we penned the cattle, we put the two-year-olds in a separate pen. On the drive to LaBelle we were near Hog Island when the stampede happened, not quite a day's drive out of LaBelle. The steers spooked, stampeded and tore down the fences, bolting in all directions. Next day we picked up strays right up to late in the afternoon. Most of 'em had stopped in a bunch when they had pretty well run themselves out, but some of the steers had run a real long distance before we caught up with them.

"After we got them all together, we had to drive them onto a one-way narrow bridge over the Caloosahatchee River. It was not easy driving wild cattle through that skinny opening, water on both sides. Cattle can spook real easy."

Being a cowboy was not always Gene Autry and Roy Rogers singing down the trail. Another misconception is that cowboys ate lots of beef. Snake remembers his father fattening a hog in the wintertime and pickling the meat in five-gallon crocks. "There was always white bacon, the side of the hog away from the bone. And we ate lots of chicken."

Roundup time meant an even more limited menu. The chuck wagon, pulled by two yokes of oxen, followed the cowboys from one set of cow pens to another as the men herded the cattle scattered over a vast expanse of unfenced grazing land. The wagon carried staples and salt pork, pots and pans. Even today Snake remembers the names of those long ago oxen teams: Blue and Brandy, Moses and Aaron.

Florida cowman. Sketch by R. Tabor, after F. Remington

The cowhands camped out in the open and the cooking was done over an open fire. As a special treat, on extended roundups, a steer would be slaughtered and the cook would smoke it. "He would cut down a myrtle bush, trim it, cut the small limbs off and hone the rest to sharp points. Then he would slice the beef into strips, skewer them on

this improvised spit, build a roaring fire and smoke them over the embers." This didn't always work out but when it did it was a rare deli-
cacy out there in the wilds.

"Back in those days before there was any improved pasture land,
the cows didn't have calves year-round like they do now. They would
mostly calve in the spring of the year. We'd start out about July for the
first roundup, mark and brand the babies and dip them. While doing
this we would also gather the beef, which means the steers. In the beginning we'd pick out the choicest-looking bulls and save them for
breeding purposes; the other bull calves we would castrate and make
steers out of them.

"There was a time-honored way of branding the calves. One man
wrestled the calf to the ground, catching him by the right hind leg,
because the branding was done on the right-hand side. The cowboy
working with you picked up the front leg as soon as you had the hind
leg and would flip him to the ground on his left side. Calves also were
earmarked because brands could be taken off or removed by rustlers.
The special cuts on the ear were permanent and identifiable."

Hunting 'Gators

The year was 1920 and people were the endangered species, not alligators! There had been a long, hot, dry spell in Charlotte County that fall, perfect weather for 'gator hunting and Snake's father knew every 'gator pond from Charlotte Harbor to the Myakka River and all over Sarasota County.

Early one morning R. J. and his son set out for four or five days of hunting the dangerous critters. They took two horses, bedrolls and a wagon with groceries, a box of salt to cure the hides and R. J.'s special 'gator pole made to order by the local blacksmith. The custom-made pole was an eighteen-foot pine sapling with an iron hook on the end.

"Alligators dig burrows in ponds; we called them caves. A 'gator usually fans out a basin in front of his cave to sun himself and during a dry spell his tracks show up in the mud. You could look at the tracks and tell pretty much the size of the gator, mostly from seven foot up to a whopping fourteen foot. Dad would run that pole down into the 'gator's cave and try to get him to bite it. Once hooked (inside his mouth so as not to damage the hide) Dad would drag him out, flailing wildly. As soon as his head cleared the water, I was ready with the ax and smashed him between the eyes."

Snake Whidden described all this in a matter-of-fact manner, but it was an undertaking obviously fraught with danger. The alligator always put up a good fight, bracing its feet against the top of its cave. It didn't emerge serenely out of the murky depths, but thrashed and swung its tail around, thrashing out at its adversary; their strength is phenomenal. Add to this the fact that venomous cottonmouth moccasins also do not like to be disturbed. They would coil themselves on the bank or lie in the water just waiting. Snake and his dad quite often were knee-deep in the water hole, yanking on the alligator and "those cotton-mouths would just coil there with an open mouth (looked like Mammoth Cave to me) and wait for you to get close enough so he could get you."

Once the gator was killed, Snake and his dad would skin it, leaving as little meat as possible, spread out the hide and salt it down so it wouldn't sour. "Then we'd roll the hides as tight as we could get them so the salt wouldn't roll out. We put them in a wooden box in the back of the wagon and covered them with damp burlap sacks. We couldn't let the sun shine on 'em because that made the scales slip off and ruined the hide." After days of hunting, the Whiddens would take the hides across the river to Punta Gorda and sell them to A. J. Kinsel who operated a tannery there.

Mary Ellen Glover Manning vividly remembers the tannery. There was a narrow-gauge ice-car track that ran parallel to King Street (northbound U.S. 41) from the ice plant on Virginia Avenue down to the docks. The ice-car was powered by a gasoline engine which delivered it to a chute at the fish houses down on the dock. Sometimes Mary Ellen and her close friend, Wanda Bassett, would hitch a ride to Wanda's house or the Glover store on this car. It was fun and saved them a lot of walking.

In this same location along the ice-car tracks, Mr. Kinsell lived in a two-story all-tin house. He cured alligator hides and made them into pocketbooks and belts. The odor of formaldehyde was overpowering to anyone walking down that part of the street.

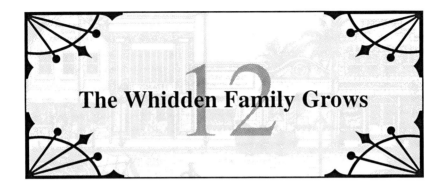

The Whidden Family Grows

Snake Whidden left the cowboy trail for a while; he wanted a change of pace and went to work in a sawmill. Eventually he came home to work the cattle for his dad and Koon. "I guess I just wanted to put my feet under Dad's table again." Snake stayed single ("I wanted to hit the high spots first") until he was twenty-five when he married Josephine Taylor and started a family, son James E. Jr. and daughter Joanne.

He was working with his dad in 1935 when the dreaded Texas tick fever hit Florida. The U.S. Department of Agriculture forced cattlemen to dip their herds every fourteen days. This was a difficult time for Snake and his dad. "Fourteen months of the hardest work we'd ever done, dipping in all sorts of weather, hot, cold or pelting rain." Finally, the epidemic was licked.

Snake's lifelong ambition was to have 1,000 head of cattle and he strove energetically toward that goal. There were many setbacks—the Texas tick fever and the horrible screwworm, but he finally reached his goal of 1,000 head of cattle in 1955, only to find that his 7,210 acres would not support that large a herd. ("You figure ten acres to the cow.") Snake started cutting back the size of his herd and at the same time sold off most of his large spread. By 1958 he had sold out completely and become a "retired" cattleman.

Snake, James E. Whidden Sr., lives on seventy acres of his former ranch, a farmland oasis surrounded by a growing commercial area of his own making. His son, Jimmy, lives nearby in a house built around the old chimney of Snake's childhood home. Jimmy is a land developer and owner of the Whidden Industrial complex in Charlotte Harbor. Snake had another son, Robert, by a later marriage to Billie Jackson. Robert works with Jimmy in his many enterprises. For eighty-six years the Whidden family has helped build Charlotte County.

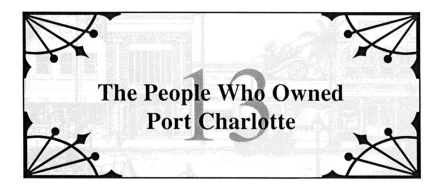

The People Who Owned Port Charlotte

We have all heard the phrase "back when Port Charlotte was A. C. Frizzell's cow pasture." Marijo Kennedy Brown, Lula Frizzell Kennedy's daughter, gave me some interesting aspects of the land and cattle baron's background. Frizzell and his wife, Pattie, were railroad telegraphers who came from Alabama in 1918. "Miss Patty" worked as a telegrapher in a little community near Murdock and A. C. in the Murdock settlement itself. When they had saved a few hundred dollars from their combined salaries they quit their jobs and bought the Murdock Mercantile store and a small boarding house. The store is still there, now a citrus shipping business next to the Murdock post office.

A. C.'s sister, Lula, came to visit and met another young railroad telegrapher, T. I. Kennedy, who had just started working at the Murdock railroad station. Love was in the air and Lula decided to prolong her visit and started helping out at the Mercantile, a typical store of that era. It carried a little bit of everything and was also the local post office. To quote Tosie Quednau Hindman, who many years later worked at the store and was the postmistress, "We sold everything from half a pound of rat cheese to a fine leather saddle!"

A. C. and Lula's parents came to join them in Murdock, settling in a big old rambling house where the Charlotte County Administrative Offices are located. Time went on and the sprawling Frizzell ranch extended from Charlotte Harbor over to the DeSoto County line, north to the Sarasota County line and then down to the Myakka River. A. C. also owned some property in Immokalee. The erstwhile telegrapher was now a land "baron." Much of his property had been acquired slowly, acre by acre, in land sold for back taxes.

26

Grayce Johnson (Mrs. Charles Myers of Port Charlotte) remembers the Frizzell ranch well. Her father, Pat Johnson, was a cowhand for A. C. Frizzell and the family lived in a cabin on the ranch. The spread was so large that her father often had to go on long trips over the range. He and other cowhands traveled by horseback, their saddlebags loaded with coffee, lard, flour or meal. They ate "off the land," cooking native creatures such as curlews, woodstorks and ironheads over an open fire. Try that menu for next Sunday's dinner!

Sometimes Grayce and her brothers would join their father on a raccoon hunt into the Big Slough for a week or more. Pat Johnson would cut cabbage palm fronds and place them over little pine saplings to form a lean-to for shelter. Palmetto fronds laid on the ground made a floor and quilts and blankets were the forerunners of sleeping bags.

The family would stay out there ten days at a time, trapping the 'coons and skinning them. "My father would make a frame out of palm tree fronds by stripping them down to the stems and running them around the edge of the skins. We would lay them against the sides of the lean-to in order to dry them in the sun." When the skins were cured, Pat Johnson would stack them and wait for a Mr. Harrington to come down from Arcadia to buy them. Grayce recalls, "That's the way we earned the money to go on a shopping spree in Punta Gorda."

Most groceries and such were bought at A. C. Frizzell's commissary on the ranch, the Mercantile Store. It was like a company store and the people who worked for Frizzell were partially paid in artificial money called "babbit," which was crudely stamped out of lead and was negotiable only at the commissary. So the raccoon money really came in handy.

With little real money to spend, people tended to stay around the ranch and make their own amusement. Charlie and Betty Slaughter were one of the ranch families who used to give cane-grinding parties. The sugar cane was ground into a mouth-watering syrup enjoyed by all. Life on the Frizzell ranch was simple, as Grayce puts it, "We didn't really have much, but it was a lovely time."

A. C. Frizzell had two nephews, Joyce and Jack Hindman, who left their home in Alabama to come live with their uncle. It was 1934, the boys were in their early teens. Joyce recalls, "There was an old, two-story, frame hotel with eighteen or twenty rooms just about where the El Jobean road comes into Route 41 now." The boys' grandmother lived in a large frame house and Jack stayed with her. Joyce lived with his uncle, Frona Frizzell, in living quarters back of the Murdock Mercantile Store, the ranch commissary.

After school Joyce helped out at the store, which sold everything from shoe polish to bridles, groceries and yard goods. There were no school buses in those days so Joyce hitched rides all the way down the Tamiami Trail across the old bridge to the Taylor Street school. Not many youngsters lived on the ranch then and for sport he used to go hunting on his uncle's range. "You could always take a bird dog, be gone an hour or so and bag a lot of quail, wild turkeys and doves."

Joyce left the ranch his senior year in high school to live in Punta Gorda, but still has happy memories of his stay at the Frizzell spread.

A. C. sold a vast tract of land, about 79,000 acres in 1954 or thereabouts—the Port Charlotte and Myakka sections—to the Mackle Brothers or Florida West Coast Land Development Company, later to become General Development Corp. His Englewood real estate went to the Vanderbilt brothers (about 20,000 acres). He was active in management until his unexpected death in 1961 at home in Murdock.

* * *

Edith Jones, who still lives in Punta Gorda, comes from a well-known local family. Her aunt, a prominent teacher in town had a school named for her: the Sallie Jones Elementary School on Cooper Street. Her father, Charles, was one of the Jones boys who owned the popular meat market and her great uncle was Luther Koon, a prosperous cattleman.

In 1940, W. Luther Koon left a large ranch (more than 16,000 acres) down in Dade County to his nephews, the Jones brothers and their sister, Sallie. It was called the Bee Ranch Cattle Company and they raised Brahman cattle. In remembering her great-uncle, Edith notes he was a large man, 6'4" and around 240 pounds. She remembers that, when a couple of those big Brahmans got into a fight. "Uncle Luther tried to separate them on his own. One of the bulls just picked him up, threw him aside, and broke his leg!"

The ranch was a big operation and the Brahmans so numerous they were widely scattered over the range. During the screwworm fly infestation in Florida, an inspector had to stay at the ranch for three months to supervise the dipping of the cattle. There were fifteen hired hands and they all came in for lunch. "Dad did the cooking. He had a crippled hip and couldn't ride so they elected him cook. Mother was smart; she wasn't about to go down there and fix lunch. The camp-out was an old schoolhouse with no hot water and no sink." Edith remembers her Uncle Neal, an avid coffee drinker, brewing it in the fields when it was 95 degrees in the shade. "He'd get a coffee can from the middle of nowhere, put some grounds in it, get some water from a nearby stream and make him a pot of coffee. You could cut it with a knife."

Ruth Stephens Allen of Cleveland has yet another recollection of the days of the big cattlemen and open ranges. One of the most exciting forms of entertainment for local children was to watch the cattle dipping. Years ago there was an infestation of spotted ticks; the Lykes brothers, big cattle grazers, held roundups to immunize their herds.

"We used to climb on top of our outhouse, which was next to the pasture, and watch the cowboys chase bulls, jump fences and bulldog 'em. Never will forget the first time I went to a rodeo. I was so disappointed. I had seen that all my life!"

The cattle business is still a prime industry in this area, but the days of the wild and woolly cowpokes, flamboyant cattlemen and land barons are now a thing of the past.

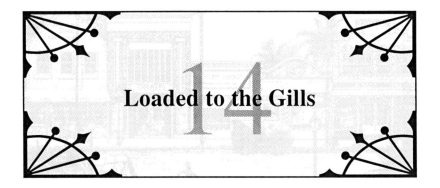

Loaded to the Gills

The Cuban fishermen and the Indians had known for a long time of the abundance of fish around the fat point of land jutting out into Charlotte Harbor. They had squatters' rights until the early settlers of Hickory Bluff began to fish the north side of the Peace River, Then came James Madison Lanier and later Colonel Isaac Trabue with his little settlement of Trabue. Fishing was plentiful around Trabue but didn't become profitable until the arrival of the railroad to the little town. Now there was a way to ship fresh-iced fish to Northern markets and a booming industry was born in the town that was now called Punta Gorda. Fish companies were formed, Chadwick Brothers, the West Coast Fish Company and the Punta Gorda Fish Company were some of them. Let's hear about those days from some of the old-timers.

When asked what life was like in Charlotte Harbor and Punta Gorda back in the early 1900s, Grant Johnson responded, "It was kind of like living out in the woods." Grant was the oldest son of Sumner and Nettie Johnson, early settlers of Fort Ogden. They came here around 1910 to live on seventy acres of what was to become Melbourne Street in Charlotte Harbor. When not building boats, he trapped this land for furs (raccoon and rabbit).

"There were two stores in Charlotte Harbor then; Mott Willis had a general store and Mr. Stephens had one with the post office in it." The mail boat would pick up the mail at this little branch and carry it across the bay to Punta Gorda where it would be sorted and the out-of-town mail put on the train. The mail boat also carried passengers at fifty cents a head. The bay was a busy place in those days since water was the only link between the two towns.

At an early age Grant went to work for T. C. Crosland's West Coast Fish Company in Punta Gorda. "We stop netted. We caught all kinds of fish. Some we could sell and some we couldn't." Catfish were out, but mullet, trout, snook and red fish were much in demand. There were five or six in the crew including the captain. "We would leave Punta Gorda and go to the mouth of the Myakka River; we'd fish that shoreline all the way from the river mouth to Turtle Bay. We couldn't go to Placida and Boca Grande Pass because they were in Lee County—they didn't let us stop net in Lee County in those days.

The men were out for a week at a time, living on a houseboat barge. Sometimes we'd go ashore and camp in the woods with the barge nearby. There were stores along the bay but we didn't buy anything that wouldn't keep—no fresh meat, but we had plenty of fish." The fish the men caught were taken immediately back to Punta Gorda by the captain. There was no refrigeration so the captain hurried back with the fresh cargo. "We would gut the red fish, trout and snook, throw the guts overboard; the gulls and pelicans following us would swoop down and have a feast." Grant notes that the captain was paid off in Punta Gorda and decided unilaterally what he would give the crew.

A fishing "Sharpie" leaving the dock for Charlotte Harbor. Sketch by R. Tabor.

At the fish dock, loading the fish on the train was an elaborate procedure in itself. "Northbound trains used to back in, near the big hotel and uncouple the passenger cars. Then the engine would back down to the fish companies on the dock. They would hook up the cars already loaded with iced fish, then back again to connect with the coach cars and take off like a ruptured duck!" There's a vivid description!

Woodrow Goff was another fisherman in those days. He and his wife, Teany, raised five children and enjoyed a comfortable living from the largesse of the sea. He had a houseboat, five net boats and two motor boats working these waters and remembers the good old days: "The railroad tracks came right out into the bay and refrigerated cars were loaded to the gills with fish. I've seen as many as seven carloads of fish go out of Punta Gorda in one day—5,000 pounds of fish to the carload. The West Coast Fish Company had a beauty of a boat, the *Sea Belle*, seventy-five feet over all. She used to go south clear to Marathon for mackerel, blue fish, pompano. Those were the days!"

Another handsome fishing boat was the *Chase*, belonging to the Florida Fish and Produce Company, operating out of Punta Gorda in 1901. At first, the schooner used only her sails for power, later, after being sold to the West Coast Fish Company, she ran by power and sail. On one trip in 1915, the fish cargo of the *Chase* amounted to 70,000 pounds! Her captain in 1919 was the teenager Fred Quednau.

Murry Hall was the skipper of one of the Punta Gorda Fish Company's boats which serviced the islands: Captiva, Useppa, Crow Key and Two Pines. These boats carried freight of all kinds, mail and passengers and on the return trip they picked up fish from the various stations in Charlotte Harbor and Pine Island Sound.

The fish were shunted down a chute from the station into the boat's hold; a deckhand on the ready with a long pole would distribute the fish evenly, port and starboard, to keep the boat on an even keel.

The man in charge of the fishing station led a lonely life, much like that of a lighthouse keeper. His home was on stilts out in the water and he couldn't leave, save in a dire emergency. He lived out his days in solitude, except for the visits of the runboats and occasional fishermen—alone with his thoughts, the cries of the seabirds and the ever present smell of fish.

* * *

Buster Crosland, son of T. C. Crosland, owner of the West Coast Fish Company has had a lifetime of experience on the runboats starting at age eleven. Every summer, as soon as school closed, the young boy would take off on trips down the bay. By the time he was in the eighth grade, he was running one of the boats for his father. He can still recall the names of the boats: the *Chase*, the *Sea Belle*, *Teddy*, *Powell* and "when dad bought the Chadwick brothers out, we had the *Ray*, *Iris* and *America*.

"We had ice houses all the way down to Patricia, Matlacha, Punta Blanco and Captiva Pass; to Black Rock, St. James City and Tarpon Bay. From there we went down to Carlos Pass and Crow Key. During the mackerel season, the run season, my dad had ice lighters, barges with refrigerator rooms on them and living quarters. Usually a man and wife would live on board. We would follow the fleet down and anchor them at different places along the coast. The first anchorage was usually Pavillion Key, then Lostmans River, Shark River and Sand Key. Dad had a fish house at Marathon on the Keys, one at Fahkahatchee down at the Ten Thousand Islands and also at Chokoloskee where we took supplies to old man Smallwood at his trading post." It was from Smallwood's trading post that Captain Fred Quednau brought back three tiny bear cubs that were to become the Crosland's family pets.

Sport Fishing in the Harbor

Another type of fishing began with the advent of the railroad, the big hotel and subsequent influx of wealthy men with time on their hands—sports fishing. Teddy Roosevelt was a great devil fish enthusiast and caught a world-record monster in these waters.

At a later date, Charlie Hurst recalls "the best tarpon fishing used to be in the river off Cleveland." The Peace River Hotel, owned by a Mr. Cahoun, was filled to capacity with amateur fishermen lured by tales of the fish to be caught in "Danforth's Pool." General Charles H. Danforth owned most of Harbour Heights at the time. The "big hole in the river" just off his property, was a choice fishing spot. This deep hole was always an ideal spot to find the great game fish, the tarpon.

Alfred Ballard worked for General Danforth, married a young Charlotte Harbor girl, Hilda Hand, and the couple lived for a while in the general's home in Harbour Heights. Alfred, who was an excellent cook, was offered a job as chef at the Allapatchee Lodge in Punta Gorda and the couple moved there. The lodge was owned by Lewis Calder, a wealthy New Yorker.

The big hotel was over a quarter century old when Sam Gibbs came to Punta Gorda more than sixty years ago. His father, Eddie, had been a farmer—cotton, corn and peanuts—in Georgia. He brought his wife, Lula, and eleven children here to start a 100-acre orange grove on Shell Creek. It was a rugged existence. At first the family lived in tents, then the 1926 storm blew them away and they were homeless. "Mr. Rockwell was starting a chicken farm and had just finished building a large chicken coop. Before the chickens moved in, we did. We lived there 'til we could build a house across the road from the grove."

Most of the children worked in the grove but Sam had a mechanical bent and went into construction work. After many years of toil and a moderate livelihood from the groves, Eddie Gibbs sold the 100 acres on Shell Creek, but he wasn't ready to retire—not by a long shot. He opened up Gibbs Pool Hall next door to Mobley's Seminole Pharmacy. It was not the type of poolroom you see these days on "Miami Vice" with lowlife characters skulking around and "narc" undercover men playing a nervous game while stalking a drug transaction. Eddie's was a spot for young people to congregate other than at the movies; a family place and Eddie Gibbs worked hard to keep it that way.

He ran the poolroom by day and moonlighted as night watchman at the hotel. His son, Sam Gibbs, remembers the old hotel as "a beautiful place, as pretty a place as you ever want to see. As many as 400 to 500 tourists stayed there in the winter and every fall they'd bring in girls from the north to work as waitresses. We young boys used to call them 'biscuit shooters.' I'll never know why the name caught on."

Hilda Hand Larrison has a vivid picture in her mind of the backstage activities of the old hotel. At an early age, Hilda went to work at the Hotel Charlotte Harbor, running the gigantic monster of a dishwashing machine. She remembers that the kitchen was huge and always full of activity: the large ranges steaming with delicious-smelling foods and the chef and his helpers running around in their big white hats. She also recalls that her stepfather used to deliver cordwood to the hotel for use in its many fireplaces.

The family of Danette Dreggors Bonnell spans a period just short of 100 years, from 1887 when our town was born, when the magnificent new hotel was completed. Danette's grandparents, the Conollys, arrived from the north.

With them was their young daughter, Louise, Danette's mother. She was fourteen years old and her father had just been hired as night clerk at the Hotel Punta Gorda. As a young teenager, she and her sisters had a great time playing in the cupola above the stately ballroom, romping through the exotic gardens and racing pell-mell over the oyster-shelled driveway and walks. It was like living in a fairyland with beautiful surroundings, wealthy and famous people strolling on the grounds and meals fit for a king.

This fairy tale ended abruptly when Louise's father died and the family had to leave their glamorous home. Mrs. Conolly, as many young widows seemed to do in those days, opened a rooming house on Marion Avenue over the Smith Bakery.

One of her roomers, a young man from Fort Ogden, Harry Dreggors, took an immediate shine to Louise and the two were married in 1903. The young couple set up housekeeping in a house Harry had built on Sullivan Street.

It was in this house that Danette Dreggors was born in 1904, a third generation Punta Gordan. She recalls that the house was surrounded by a pineapple pinery, a prime business in the town's earlier days. She also remembers that Virginia Avenue was nothing more than a weed ridden, dirt, cart path. Danette Dreggors Bonnell, now a widow, lives in a small apartment in her old family home, not far from her nephew, Cecil Keen, and his two daughters. They comprise the fourth and fifth generations of this Punta Gorda family.

The growth of Punta Gorda was accelerated by the presence of the big old hotel, first as the Hotel Punta Gorda, later after Collier's remodeling as the Hotel Charlotte Harbor. Not only did shops spring up but professional men began to hang out their shingles as doctors or lawyers. Earl Farr, a young man newly graduated from the University of Florida Law School and eager to start his practice arrived here in the 1920s from Wauchula. He had "scouted" Fort Lauderdale, Winter Haven and Punta Gorda, "all fine places to support a law practice, but the best fishing in Florida, to my way of thinking, was in Punta Gorda." Mr. Farr, one of our most eminent attorneys is also an inveterate sportsman with a delightfully dry sense of humor. His wife, Sue, recalled fondly the opulence of the old hotel, the spacious rooms, the delicious meals and exquisite service. "Earl and I traveled to Europe many times and didn't see anything to compare with the splendor in which the meals were served."

The chef not only prepared epicurean delights, but enhanced them on the buffet table with ice sculptures: a swan, a Valentine's Day heart, a sailing ship or a leaping fish. Every time a child had a birthday, the party was usually held on the hotel's beachfront at the umbrella tables or elsewhere on the hotel grounds. Grown-up parties were held at the hotel as well and were dressy, sumptuous affairs in the ballroom after delicious dinners concocted by the temperamental chef.

Emmett Perkins and his wife, Ruth, were one of the many couples who enjoyed the social activities in the hotel. One of Ruth's fondest memories is of Mr. Alford's New Year's Eve parties. Everybody dressed to the teeth. "Mr. and Mrs. Alford, a charming couple, circulated among the guests, greeting one and all. The food was delicious and the ice sculptures were works of art."

Tosie Hindman, daughter of Cap'n Fred and Belle Quednau, used to play in the old hotel with a close friend, Mary Alford, daughter of the owner. The two girls loved to run down the rambling halls, play hide and seek in the multitude of closets, cupboards and storage rooms and ride in the elevator, the only one in town! One memorable day they somehow managed to get stuck between floors and had to be pulled out through the roof of the elevator. This experience was almost as unnerving to our Tosie as the time she fell off Cap'n Fred's boat at the dock in Useppa!

Tosie gave me such a unique description of the old hotel that I'd like to share it with you. "It reminded me of a prissy little girl, lots of warm colors, lots of yellow, sunshiny and bright, just bubbling all over. The ballroom had a dome ceiling and you could look at the stars at night. Huge mirrors with gold trim reflected the dancers." One can picture those two young girls, eyes like saucers, peering around the corner of the ballroom, watching the grown-up fairyland.

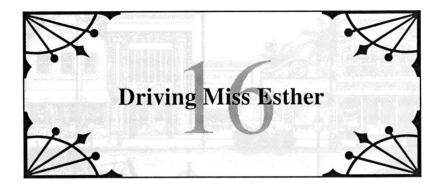

Driving Miss Esther

The social life in our little town was beginning to grow, as Mrs. Esther McCullough gently chided me on our first interview. "Punta Gorda wasn't just ranchers, cowboys and fishermen." In the early 1900s, the town was surprisingly cosmopolitan despite its size. The Hotel Punta Gorda drew many diversified and sophisticated patrons—some of whom, like Mr. Perry McAdow, Albert W. Gilchrist, the Colt family and Colonel Pepper decided to make their home here. There was a busy social life and "Miss Esther," a charming lady in every way, was kind enough to share some of these memories with me.

Miss Esther's father, the Reverend B. F. Oswald, retired from the Methodist ministry and came here from Ohio with his son in 1913. They settled in the rural community of Solana, near Punta Gorda and Esther and her mother followed in 1914 after Esther's high school graduation at the age of sixteen.

The pretty young girl soon became a popular member of the younger set of Punta Gorda, joining various clubs that were sprouting up in the growing town and going to dances in the Hotel Punta Gorda. "Cars were practically nonexistent, only a select few such as Mr. McAdow owned one. The day his driver had a wreck Mr. McAdow stored the car in his garage and never used it again!"

Two venerable old Buicks served as taxis in town but most families still used their horse and buggy or bicycles. Miss Esther remembers entire families setting off down the road on their bikes and quite a bit of walking was done, not as a physical fitness project, but from sheer necessity. As a young girl, she often walked to town from her home in Solana.

Adrian Jordan had arrived in town a few years before the Oswalds and purchased the *Punta Gorda Herald* in 1901. Mr. Jordan had two sons, Vernon and Julian, who were studying dentistry. To help defray their college expenses, the two young men opened the first picture show in town. They rented a building on Marion Avenue, put in some kitchen chairs and a piano and they were in business. The boys showed early silent movies and between reels, a friend, Grace Dewey, sang. They did fairly well and sold the business to Harry Goldstein and Emmett Perkins. With that money, they both went off to school and eventually became practicing dentists. A third son, Adrian C., would follow his father in the newspaper business.

Vernon was instantly attracted to the pretty new arrival from Ohio. The two had met at a bridge party held at the home of J. N. Sykes on Taylor Street. She was sixteen and he was twenty-eight. A fervent courtship followed, but Esther had enough sense to realize she was too young and made him wait five years before they were married.

Meanwhile, one of Esther's friends, Sara Boyle, a teacher in a little country school in Iowa, wanted to go on to higher education. Examinations for teachers' certificates were being held in Arcadia that year (1914) and she asked Esther to go with her. "My father thought I might as well take the exam too, since I was just out of school and it was all fresh in my mind."

The two young women stayed at the Arcadia House for a week of exams which both girls passed. While they were there, the county superintendent of schools came to the hotel and interviewed Esther. He must have been impressed because a short time later a letter arrived asking Esther to teach the first four grades in the Charlotte Harbor School—this at the age of sixteen!

"The Lord was with me. The woman who had the other grades was a graduate of a New York Normal School. She was an intelligent lady but poor in mathematics. We roomed together and I would work out her arithmetic problems for the next day. She was an excellent teacher and, in return, helped me in countless ways."

Esther boarded with the Gidden family in Charlotte Harbor, old settlers with a lovely home on the waterfront. "Mrs. Gidden was a grand cook and we ate with handsome sterling silver every meal, even breakfast!" The young teacher spent the school week with this family since the only way to reach Punta Gorda and Solana was by boat. Esther went over on the early mail boat Monday morning and a special boat came for her on Friday because she always had a date on Friday night, usually with Vernon Jordan. These dates often involved a picture show. One of Esther's favorites was "The Perils of Pauline."

The early Charlotte Harbor schoolhouse was an old two-story building made of rough lumber. There were only two rooms with a partition down the middle. Hogs ran through the sandy yard and clustered under the schoolhouse in the hot lazy days. A fence with a stile surrounded the building to keep out roaming cattle. Esther's salary was $50 a month and, when she was promoted to principal at the age of seventeen, she received a raise of $15 a month.

After five years of courtship Esther finally said, "I do" to her persistent beau, Dr. Vernon Jordan, and settled into life as a young matron in town. There were plenty of clubs and activities to fill her days. There were afternoon bridge clubs for which the ladies dressed up "like Mrs. Astor's plug horse." Esther fondly remembers one of her favorite outfits. "It was a black dress with blue-edged panels offsetting a pale blue crepe de chine underskirt. With it, I wore a black lace hat trimmed with sequins and long white gloves. Believe it or not, I wasn't overdressed!"

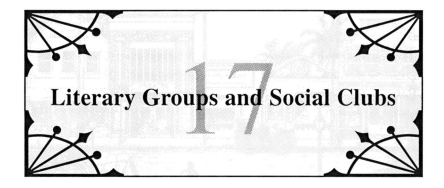

Literary Groups and Social Clubs

An eminent resident of the town was "Colonel" John Charles Pepper who had practiced law for forty years in Illinois and retired to our town in 1896. An impressive home was built for the Pepper family on the corner of Retta Esplanade and Cross Street.

Rupert Carpenter Guthrie, whose childhood encompassed both sides of the river, Charlotte Harbor and Punta Gorda, remembers the home well. We always called it the 'wrong-side-out house.' It was of English architecture with the joists and stringers exposed on the outside. Esther recalls the interior of the house as it was when the colonel lived there with three of his four daughters, one of whom was the legendary teacher, Miss Norma Pepper.

"It was a lovely home and when the family moved down here, they brought a live-in maid with them. The living room was large and filled with red velvet Victorian furniture. The library was crammed with books from floor to ceiling; a Franklin stove heated the room. This is where the Fortnightly Club met on Tuesdays and read Shakespeare." This literary group met in the homes of the members and "did more actual cultural work than any club I've been in since. The members were intellectually hungry, you might say, educated women who took turns writing informative papers on various subjects."

There was also the Music and Expression Club, just for young folk who met at the home of Mrs. J. F. Corbett. The location for this gathering was at the corner of Olympia Avenue and Sullivan Street in a home originally built by Mr. Hart, maternal grandfather of Frank and Leo Wotitzky. "Once a week we went there; they were great on expression here, because Miss Norma Pepper read beautifully. Henry Farrington's sister Helen was a pupil of hers and went on to teach it at the college level."

Still another club was called The Married Ladies' Social Club. It met in the homes of members and was strictly "a dress-up and go-to eat" club; the Fortnightly Club more or less looked down their noses at them.

Last but not least was the Punta Gorda Civic Association which met in the city hall, a small cement block building on the site of the present one. This was a group of ladies interested in the welfare of the community as a whole. One of their first projects was a campaign to get the cows off the streets. Their flowers and shrubbery were being trampled into the ground. Senator Cooper's wife was most ardent in this endeavor since she had one of the most beautiful gardens in town, filled with lilies and other exotic blooms.

Mrs. J. H. Hancock was another supporter of this cause, as was Esther's mother-in-law, Mrs. Jordan, who had erected a tall fence around their property to keep the cattle out. Cows were not the sole nuisance. Joe Addison's pony ran loose through the streets, as did Kathrine Stewart's pet fawn.

In 1925 these three clubs, the Fortnightly Club, the Music and Expression Club and the Married Ladies' Social Club merged to form the Punta Gorda Women's Club.

Other organizations in town were the Eastern Star, Woodmen of the World, the Myakka Order of Red Men and the Masons. The latter was by far the largest of the fraternal organizations, having a spacious Masonic Hall on Sullivan Street. It was a two-story building complete with a library presided over by a Mrs. Gould. Miss Esther reports: "We usually had our dances in the big hotel, but when it was closed for the summer we used the Masonic Hall.

"In spite of the heat, ladies really dressed up in Punta Gorda in those days, even for the afternoon parties. My mother-in-law, with an Irish sense of humor used to say, 'Pride knows neither heat or cold.' Most of us bought our clothes at Seward's, an exclusive ladies' dress shop. Mrs. Seward was an aunt of the Wotitzky boys."

Esther and Dr. Jordan were married for twenty-four years and during some of those years she taught in Punta Gorda. Among her pupils were Leo Wotitzky and Nathaniel "Doc" McQueen. When Dr. Jordan died, Miss Esther remained in Punta Gorda close to all her old and cherished friends. One of these, Sam "Mac" McCullough, she later married. Miss Esther saw many changes in the town. She remembered fondly "the strange paradox of the Fortnightly Club reciting Shakespeare while cows were staked out downtown."

The Smell of Chalk and Blackberry Cobbler

Shortly after Colonel John C. Pepper moved his family here in 1896, his daughter, Norma, opened a private school in a one-room house near Herald Court. The school encompassed all grades up to and including the twelfth. Miss Norma Pepper was an intelligent woman with a keen sense of humor and an avid desire to teach. When the hurricane of 1910 demolished her building, she continued to teach for a short time in the parlor of her home.

With the Taylor Street School finally completed, Miss Norma Pepper became both a first-grade teacher and a legend. Leo Wotitzky, one of our town's leading attorneys and one of her pupils, notes that "she taught just about everybody who grew up in Punta Gorda."

Nathaniel "Doc" McQueen, the son of one of the first doctors in town, had a fond and vivid memory of Miss Pepper and the town. "In my early childhood there were no paved streets and only one sidewalk on part of Marion Avenue. The first asphalt paved roads were on Marion Avenue from where the hospital is now, through downtown and out to Berry Street. Taylor was paved only as far as the schoolhouse.

"When I went to school," Doc recalled, "Miss Norma Pepper was my first teacher. She was a little gray-haired lady, tiny and sort of stooped and she carried a big palmetto switch. She'd hit that blackboard a real whack to get your attention." When asked if the switch was ever used for discipline, Doc replied, "No, she didn't have to! She was a forceful lady and she could stare a hole in you."

Doc can recall some of those early lessons about upper and lower case letters by heart. "When you go to the circus," Miss Pepper would say, "The little children sit in the front row and back of them are the big folks, the lower case and capital letters. Little children—abcd, BIG FOLKS—ABCD. After seventy years, I've never forgotten that; it's what made Miss Norma Pepper the fine teacher that she was."

Another one of Miss Norma Pepper's pupils was Minta Harper Hopper Harder. Calvin Monroe Hopper brought his family here from Breckenridge, Texas, in 1913; Minta was nine years old, her younger sister, Ethel, six. All the family chattel, including furniture, two teams of mules, chickens and the hired hand came by boxcar; the Hoppers came by passenger train.

After a short stay in Punta Gorda, Calvin bought a 160-acre homestead in neighboring Cleveland and moved his family there. To supplement his income from the ranch, he used his mule teams to haul oranges from the various groves to the boxcars. Minta's mother, Rose, contributed to the family income by teaching in Cleveland, Charlotte Harbor, Punta Gorda and Acline. When teaching in Charlotte Harbor, Rose had to leave home before dawn; Calvin would drive her by mule team to meet the early mail boat. In the late afternoon, husband, mules and children would await her return. It took a plucky woman to teach under these conditions and raise a family besides.

When Minta graduated from Charlotte High School out of a class of eight, she was the first girl to receive a state scholarship for teaching. After graduating from Florida State College for Women (Florida State University) she taught one year at Lake Butler and then returned home. Mathematics was her "strong point"; she taught plane geometry, math, algebra 1 and 2. "and any other teaching they needed someone to do."

It was the beginning of the Great Depression and times were very hard. Minta remembers that the teachers received a portion of their salary in script, which they traded with merchants for food and other essentials.

While she was teaching at Charlotte High, Minta met a young barber, Willie Harper, who had just opened his own shop in town; shaves were ten cents, haircuts, a quarter! Love blossomed. Minta and Willie were married but Minta lost her job. During those difficult times in Punta Gorda, a married woman wasn't allowed to teach if her husband was employed; that's how bad things were. "It was a terrible time; my husband wasn't making any money." By now, the Harpers had become a family with the birth of a daughter and there were three mouths to feed. Minta learned of a position teaching French in Crawfordville. Taking the couple's year-old daughter with her, Minta taught there for two years. "I had only two years of French and it was a struggle to keep ahead of the class!" She also taught history and math.

The young mother and wife returned to Punta Gorda when married women were permitted to teach again and remained a teacher here for thirty-eight years, retiring in 1968.

Another teacher during those lean years was Leo Wotitzky, now a well-known attorney in town. His family, originally from New York, had arrived in Punta Gorda in the late 1800s. They came, with all their family belongings, in a railroad boxcar and got off at Punta Gorda simply because it was the end of the line.

Jacob Wotitzky started a general merchandise store on Marion Avenue west of Sullivan Street. By general merchandise, says Leo, "They sold a little bit of everything." Jacob was one of the first merchants in town and did a brisk business. Later on his son, Ed, (the father of Frank and Leo) took over the business, extending it to many of the islands surrounding the area, even as far south as Miami. He sold his wares by sailing to the isolated settlers.

At about the same time a Mr. Hart owned a large store on Retta Esplanade and his business flourished until a devastating fire razed the building, which was not insured. Unnerved by this disaster, the Hart family returned to their native Philadelphia and their former life there. Their daughter, Celia, later returned to Punta Gorda as a young lady, met and married Edward Wotitzky. She was Frank and Leo's mother.

From the first grade, where Leo was taught by the legendary Miss Norma Pepper, all the way through school, he was a hard-working student. After graduating from Charlotte High School, the young man entered the University of Florida.

He had dreams of becoming a lawyer but, with insufficient funds for law school, he turned to another field, education. His first teaching job was in Crescent City, where he earned the magnificent sum of $85 a month. "There were two months when they couldn't pay me and the only thing that kept me from starving to death was the kind lady who ran the boarding house where I stayed. She took pity on me and saw that I was fed until I got some back pay!"

Leo returned home to Punta Gorda and taught math and science in the high school. To augment his meager teaching salary, he went to work for the *Punta Gorda Herald* as a printer's devil and eventually worked up to editor.

The early '30s saw Leo in Baltimore in a civil service position helping to set up the social security system. Later on, even before finally earning his law degree, he served for twelve years as a member of the Florida Legislature from Charlotte County. Leo helped revolutionize public education through a more thorough teacher training program and an increase in teachers' salaries, a need he had experienced personally. By 1940 he had returned to teaching and for many years served as a legislator, editor of the paper and teacher all at the same time. "I had to do a lot of different jobs to make a living."

While working at the *Punta Gorda Herald*, Leo, trying to lure qualified teachers here, had compiled an elaborate brochure depicting the advantages of teaching in our fair city. There were pictures of the old hotel, views of the harbor and a scenario that described Punta Gorda as a tropical paradise.

Among the many applicants intrigued by this brochure was a pretty young teacher who sent in her application accompanied by a photograph. Leo often dropped by the school superintendent's office to check the response to his pamphlet. Upon seeing this young lady's picture, Leo remarked to the superintendent, "You ought to hire this one!" Yes, you've guessed it. The young lady was hired to teach home economics at Charlotte High School and later became Leo's wife, Zena.

In 1950 Leo realized his dream and entered the University of Florida Law School and in 1953 another dream was realized when he and Zena were married. The happy couple settled in Punta Gorda where Leo joined his brother Frank's law office. For thirty-two years the law firm has grown, expanded and prospered. Who says brothers can't get along?

Charles Jones, marshal of Bartow, Florida, was only thirty-eight years old when he died of malaria, leaving a young widow and four children. Mrs. Jones' brother, W. Luther Koon (cattleman and rancher) lived in Punta Gorda and she moved her family there to be near him.

To help make ends meet, the young mother sewed for the townsfolk and worked as a practical nurse for Dr. David Norman McQueen's patients. Her brother, of course, aided the little family financially, too.

Sallie, the only girl, was barely five years old when the family arrived but already held her own with her three brothers, Charlie, Ferg and Neal (later to become owners of the Jones Brothers Meat Market). Sallie was a happy, outgoing child with a great zest for life and learning. In those days Punta Gorda was still a very small town with fishing and cattle the main industries and the streets were paved with oyster shells from the bay. Picturesque as it was, between the cattle, fish and strewn oyster shells, there were always swarms of flies in town. This was probably one of the reasons for the typhoid epidemic that hit the town while Sallie was growing up. The young girl was fortunate enough to be among those who escaped the dreaded disease.

Sallie started school on Goldstein Street in a building that has since been converted to apartments and finished high school at the Taylor Street School. Interested in teaching, she took the state teachers' exam and received a certificate. She taught first in Chokoloskee and then Pine Island before coming home to Punta Gorda. She taught the lower grades here and then transferred to teaching high school history in 1929.

Always in the back of "Miss Sallie's" mind was a determination to get a college degree. She accomplished this by attending Florida Southern College during the summer months when she wasn't teaching. During this period, Miss Sallie fell in love with a young collegian and they became engaged. Tragically, he was killed in an automobile accident and Miss Sallie never married. From then on Sallie Jones devoted her life to education.

Edith Jones speaks fondly of her aunt. "She was a bushel of fun and loved to entertain us. She played games with us, sang to us and took us to the movies and the beach—anywhere we wanted to go. She was dedicated to education. Her whole life was teaching."

In 1938, "Miss Sallie," as she was affectionately known, was elected county superintendent of schools, the first woman to hold that position in the state of Florida. She was a popular superintendent—her office was always open to everyone. She began the first school lunchroom program and established the policy that all teachers be qualified in their special fields. Miss Sallie was respected by all and became a good-will ambassador between school and community. She retired in 1953.

Our little town was growing by leaps and bounds and a new elementary school was built in 1956. At that time it was suggested that the school be named in honor of the beloved Miss Sallie. The school board agreed and in 1959 the building was officially dedicated as the Sallie Jones Elementary School. Miss Sallie, terminally ill, was unable to attend the ceremonies but was there in spirit. She passed away the following year, leaving an indelible mark on the education system of Charlotte County.

Jesse Knight, the great-grandfather of Gladys Roberts Wilt, was one of the first "big" cattlemen in the state and founded Knight's Station east of Tampa. Her grandfather, Shadrick "Shade" Hancock was also a cattleman who settled in the Myakka area, driving his cattle along a trail blazed by cattleman Ziba King (King's Highway) south to the Peace River. Shade also built three churches around the Myakka area and a schoolhouse for itinerant teachers.

One of his daughters, Mary Frances, was a woman ahead of her time. In an era when most young girls stayed home until they married, Mary Frances taught school. Through her father's encouragement to learn, she was able to get a teaching certificate. She taught in Bee Ridge, probably named because anything over three-feet high in Florida is called a ridge and there were beehives there.

In 1898 Mary Francis married Mitchell Roberts whose family had left Georgia during the great Depression of 1892 and settled in Bradentown, as it was called then. The newlyweds stayed in the area for a while, started a family and eventually migrated to Punta Gorda where their last two children were born. When Mitchell learned that the railroad was planning to open up the region (later to become Murdock) to facilitate the shipping of phosphate to Boca Grande, he decided to move his family there. He reasoned that he could raise produce there and the location would be ideal for shipping it to the northern markets.

There was one drawback to this move; there was no school near Murdock. The three youngest weren't affected by this for a while. Gladys, the next to youngest, was only two-and-a-half-years-old at the time. However, Mary Frances attacked this newest problem with her usual fervor. She tutored all of them with an unflagging enthusiasm and dedication with the result that, when a school was finally opened, Gladys, then eight, entered the second grade.

This first school was held in a room of Mr. Murdock's hotel and had one teacher for all grades. The little girl walked "through fields of blue violets and wild iris" to school. It was a happy time for the youngster. Although Mitchell Roberts did fairly well with his produce business "there was not much cash money but I never felt underprivileged."

When Gladys was ready to enter the seventh grade, the family moved back to Punta Gorda amid many sad tears on Gladys' part.

She had loved living in Murdock. She attended the Taylor Street School and was a member of the first graduating class of Punta Gorda High School in 1927. Graduation exercises were held in the new building later to be called Charlotte Senior High School. Gladys was editor of the school's first annual, "The Silver King."

Her mother's love of teaching inspired Gladys to major in education; later she taught for three years in Nokomis and Boca Grande. An urge to see something of the outside world led her to visit a sister in New York City for a year. Her teaching certificate was not valid in New York, but she was lucky to find employment at various jobs. "The Depression was rampant, businessmen were selling apples on the street corners and there were soup lines in Times Square."

Arriving back home after a year in the big city, Gladys taught fourth grade in Punta Gorda and remembers that one of her pupils was Tosie Quednau (Hindman). It turned out to be an eventful year. After the initial six months, the school superintendent called a special meeting of all teachers. He announced to his stunned audience that neither the county nor the state had enough money to finish out the school year! There was nothing to do but close the school. Gladys, (shades of her mother's ingenuity) had an idea. She suggested that the faculty continue to teach for one more month without pay. The program would be accelerated to prepare the children for their next grade. All the teachers agreed to this plan and the youngsters finished their classes at a stepped-up pace. The following year the necessary funds became available and school opened on schedule.

"Doc McQueen's responsible for my coming to Punta Gorda." That was Bernice Blacklock Rountree's answer to my question of why she came here in 1937. Bernice's father, Raymond Blacklock, was connected with the University of Florida and Doc, as Charlotte County agricultural agent, had met him and become a friend of the family. Bernice, who taught school in Perry in northern Florida, was home on a visit when Doc dropped in for dinner. In the course of the evening Doc mentioned there was an opening for a home economics teacher in Punta Gorda, if Bernice was interested. Later, an interview was set up in Bradenton with Miss Sallie Jones and Bernice was hired to teach at Charlotte High School.

The McQueen family owned an apartment house on Olympia Avenue and Bernice stayed there. She remembers Miss Hattie Huested, city clerk, managed the place, which was filled with teachers except for one couple, the Hyatts, and Miss Hattie. Bernice taught seventh grade science, ninth grade English, all home economic classes and ran the school lunchroom. "I used my advanced home economics students to prepare and serve the food; they received extra credits for this. The menu was simple: hamburgers, hot dogs and cold drinks." Among the cold drinks served was Coca-Cola and the truck delivering it to the lunchroom was driven by Ebbie Rountree. Ebby and his brother, Erwin, had the local franchise. Soon Bernice and Ebby were "an item."

"There was a great girls' basketball team in school at that time and I had to ride the bus with them when they traveled out of town; I also took tickets at the football games—a teacher was jack-of-all-trades in those days for $126 a month!"

The town was still small enough so that the teachers all knew each other and were friends. Many of them, like Bernice, dated local boys. Lucille McQueen introduced her brother, Doc, to a fellow teacher, Margaret Brabson. There were dates at Desguin's Movie Theater, dinner parties, trips to Chadwick's Beach (Englewood) where there was a pavilion for dancing. Bernice Blacklock and Ebby Rountree were eventually married, as were Doc McQueen and Margaret Brabson.

Bernice stopped working after her marriage except for occasional substitute teaching. Even that came to an end with the birth of a daughter, Adelia, in 1941. In 1947 Bernice returned to full-time teaching and remained a teacher until her retirement in June of 1974. Ebby retired in 1971 and they continued to live in Punta Gorda.

Violet Harner is not a native Punta Gordan, but she and her husband looked upon the little town as their second home, spending the winters here from the 1920s on.

They grew to love the "little fishing village" and every winter they drove their house trailer into a rented spot in the municipal trailer park, now Laishley Park. Even in 1946 Punta Gorda was still small. The post office was still in the arcade and the Seminole Pharmacy still did a thriving business. That particular drugstore stands out in Mrs. Harner's mind because of the excellent ice cream and because the Mobley brothers always wore black hats and white shirts!

In 1946, the Harners spent the entire school year here because Violet had accepted a position teaching fourth grade, which was then located in the Charlotte High School. By an unusual happenstance, the Harners' only son, Lloyd, attended the same school as a high school freshman. Miss Sallie Jones was county superintendent of schools at that time and had made several improvements in the school system. She was instrumental in bringing about a closer relationship between school and community.

It was under this system that Violet Harner taught her first year in Punta Gorda. She recalls that, if a child was absent for more than a few days, the teacher was required to visit the home and find out what the problem was. Mrs. Harner also recalls that in those days, the students not only received a good broad education, but ate bountiful lunches as well.

"The cafeteria workers and some volunteer mothers canned all the fresh fruits and vegetables for the daily meal. There was no such thing as free meals then, but they didn't cost much and they were good, home-made ones." She also remembers, in particular, a weekly treat of black-berry cobbler!

The Harners moved here permanently in 1958, building a home in Port Charlotte off Conway Boulevard. Mrs. Harner taught at the Sallie Jones school in Punta Gorda for the next fifteen years. There were no longer ladies canning in the kitchen. Federal aid had entered the picture; there were free lunches amid a fast-food atmosphere.

In her last three years of teaching, Mrs. Harner devoted many hours to a reading lab for exceptional children. After retiring, she made her home in bustling Port Charlotte with her memories of quieter days amid the smell of chalk mixed with the delightful aroma of homemade blackberry cobbler.

What could be more fitting than a teacher living in a converted school house. Lonnie Friday Persons' lovely home on Virginia Avenue in Punta Gorda was once a school house in Bermont and, to add to the coincidence, she attended that school as a little girl living in Rouxville, now known as Babcock Ranch! Her father, Otto Friday, was bookkeeper and manager of the ranch and the family lived twenty-five miles from town out in the woods. By the time Lonnie was in the ninth grade, the family moved to Punta Gorda and the young girl attended Charlotte High.

During World War II, Lonnie attended Florida State College for Women in Tallahassee (Florida State) and remembers that her parents couldn't drive her home on vacations because of gas rationing. When she went home on visits, she took a bus always crowded with servicemen. She recalls one trip back to school when she had to stand all the way to Tampa. Her college roommate was Betty Jo Guthrie, who became her sister-in-law, when she married Lonnie's brother, Judge Elmer Friday.

Her first teaching job was in Frostproof, Florida. She taught third grade there and lived in a special boarding house for teachers. After a year, she was back home in Punta Gorda where she began dating Jimmy Persons and in 1948 they were married.

After time out for motherhood, Lonnie taught first at the Taylor Street School and then at Sallie Jones. One of her early pupils was Terry Knecht Dozier, 1985 National Teacher of the Year. Lonnie remembered Terry as a bright and inquisitive child, always on the go. Lonnie, retired from teaching in 1985 to enjoy the leisure life in her own schoolhouse.

Many of Punta Gorda's "old families" have produced teachers. One of them is Mary Agnes Crosland Fambrough, the granddaughter of William Monson Whitten, the pineapple pioneer, and daughter of T. C. Crosland, owner of the West Coast Fish Company. Mary Agnes later married Charles Fambrough whose family came here from Bartow. Another old family teacher is Marijo Kennedy Brown, the daughter of Lula Frizzell Kennedy and Tilly Kennedy and niece of A. C. Frizzell, the land and cattle baron. Marijo married James Brown, who at one time was the owner of the Brown Machine Company of Punta Gorda.

Still another teacher is Ethel Hopper Berhardt, the daughter of Calvin Hopper and Rose Hopper. Rose was one of the early teachers in this area and Ethel's sister is Minta Hopper Harper who was also a teacher. The family began their contributions to the education of the young of Charlotte County in 1913.

The year 1873 brought the firsts to the portion of Manatee County later to become Charlotte County—the first church and the first public school. The Trinity Methodist Church in Charlotte Harbor housed the school and, although crude at best with a thatched roof, it served its students well.

In Trabue the first public school was also part church, part school; a small wooden building where the First Methodist Church now stands. The turn of the century saw Miss Norma Pepper opening her own private school in Punta Gorda and a bit later, Mrs. Honeywell opened a Seventh-day Adventist school on Cross Street.

The first complete high school in Punta Gorda, with all twelve grades, was on Goldstein Street. U. S. Whiteaker (U. S. Cleveland's grandfather) was assistant principal and little Belle McBean (Quednau) lived right next door. The old building is still there, renovated into an apartment house.

Later on, Professor Whiteaker drew up plans for what was to become the Taylor Street School; that building was finished around 1909. It was a block structure and housed all twelve grades. At its inception the school was heated by a potbellied stove, kindling wood stacked nearby. The school yard was divided into two sections, one for the boys and the other for the girls. In the beginning there were privies in the yard, later on wooden buildings were added and inside toilets. This school served the community for fifty or more years until it was destroyed by fire.

The last high school graduation from the Taylor Street school was in 1926. After that the primary and intermediate grades remained there but the junior and senior high school classes moved to the new three-story brick building on Cooper Street, the Charlotte Senior High School.

Later, other schools were built: Sallie Jones Elementary School, East Elementary School and the Punta Gorda Junior High School added to the town's educational facilities.

In the very beginning of our town, the black community sadly lacked any educational facilities, but help was on the way! Benjamin Joshua Baker, born in 1872 in Suwannee County, was one of the first blacks to take the required teaching examination in Lake City. At age nineteen, he passed the test with flying colors and proceeded to teach for the next eleven years.

In 1902 he arrived in Punta Gorda and started a school at the intersection of Mary and Cooper streets. The Baker Academy educated two generations of children in the two-room frame building where the Cooper Street Recreational Center now stands. Later the school was moved to Charlotte Avenue, and four classrooms, restrooms, a cafeteria and an administration office were added. Because of segregation, after graduating from Baker Academy, black high school students were bused to a black high school in Fort Myers.

When Benjamin J. Baker retired, he became the first black teacher to receive the benefits of the teacher's retirement bill. This dedicated man died in 1942 before integration and its subsequent changes. He was a dedicated man and contributed a great deal to the betterment of the black community in our town.

Now, I did promise that this book would not be a historical tome, so let's introduce a little levity here with comments from some of the town's outstanding citizens.

Mention of the Charlotte Harbor School (now Schoolhouse Square in Charlotte Harbor) evokes these memories from Christine "Pat" Durrance Donald whose grandfather, Francis Durrance was the first Methodist minister in Punta Gorda. (Durrance Street is named in his honor.) Pat's family home became a restaurant (located approximately one block east of U.S. 41 on Melbourne Street), but when it was still home to little Pat, she walked through the fields to school carrying her lunch bucket. The school principal was Mr. Stroud and the teachers were all women.

There were four grades in one room and the three Rs were emphatically stressed. "We had old-fashioned teachers who believed children should learn those basic things thoroughly. If the whole room went twenty days without an absence, we were given a day off to play in the woods where Port Charlotte is now, swing on the grapevines and have a picnic. If anyone missed a day, the rest of us wanted to kill him!"

The children used to eat their lunches under the shade trees in the school yard. "The janitor was a lady, Mrs. Barrett, who lived across the street. I would often go over and have my lunch with her—we were good friends. She had a gadget for making quilts; she would pull it down from the parlor ceiling. I used to munch my lunch and watch her with fascination as she worked away at all those beautiful handmade quilts." After eating, the youngsters would play softball and volleyball until time to go back and tackle the three Rs again.

Rupert Carpenter Guthrie, whose uncle Will was one of the founders of the Punta Gorda Fish Company remembers the names of his teachers at Charlotte Harbor: Mr. Stroud, principal, Mrs. Knight and Mrs. O'Haver, teachers. "I walked to school; we children had our own paths, which wound through the woods. At recess we played games like Come Through in which everyone locked hands and you ran at them, trying to break through!" They played baseball and there were seesaws and swings in the school yard.

Bertha Mae Williams Powell was born in 1907 near Lake Butler on the "upper edge" of Florida, but her sharecropper father soon moved the family to Wauchula where she spent her early childhood. Later the family moved again—to Punta Gorda, settling "way out in the country near where the Aqui Esta shopping mall is today."

Carrying her lunch in a basket, Bertha Mae walked along the railroad tracks to the Taylor Street School (in 1920 there was no Tamiami Trail). High school classes were held upstairs and the grammar school was on the lower floor. The heating system was a wood stove and the school yard was divided down the middle by a board fence; girls played on one side, the boys on the other. In this segregated fashion they played games such as London Bridge, Merry-go-round and Stick Frog (mumblety-peg).

There were privies in the back of the school yard and Bertha Mae remembers with a chuckle the perils of using them. A Mr. Lancaster cleaned them regularly with lime, but he had no set schedule and there was no telling when he would come by in his wagon to unload the lime. It was best not to be caught unawares! The school day was long——from eight to three—with a recess for lunch from a pail or basket, and then the long trudge home along the tracks.

Sidney Parker, a well-known contractor in town, was born on a farm his parents owned near the Charlotte High School. He remembers when alligators went to school in Punta Gorda. Sidney, Ted Alexander and other friends used to bring their pet 'gators to school on a leash and stash them in the overflow troughs of the old drinking fountain.

With enough water to be comfortable, the baby swamp denizens lazed away the school day while their owners toiled at their books. To Sidney's knowledge, none of these unscholarly creatures ever got loose or caused panic in the classroom.

The children of Mack and Mary Maxwell (Maxwell's Drug Store) attended the local schools—Taylor Street and then Charlotte High. Mary made a visit one day to the old block building where her son, Richard, was a student. She climbed the wooden stairway to his classroom and was horrified to see that the potbellied stove heating the room was red hot way up to the chimney. She recognized a potential fire hazard and was even more appalled to see stacks of kindling wood stored underneath the wooden stairs. The stove had to remain for heat, but Mary saw to it that in the future, the kindling was stored outside.

Eventually, the Taylor Street School did burn to the ground. The fire occurred on a school day, but fortunately there was a small touring circus in town that day and the children had been allowed to attend it. Otherwise the youngsters would have been in school and there might have been a terrible tragedy.

Thomas "Buster" Crosland, grandson of the pineapple pioneer, William Monson Whitten, and son of T. C. Crosland, owner of the West Coast Fish Company, attended Charlotte High School when it was "brand-new." His was the class of 1932 and there were an even dozen students: nine girls and three boys. The girls enjoyed having the boys in class and elected them to the three top offices. Buster was president, Bill Roberts, vice-president and Custer Rowland was secretary-treasurer. They were the first graduating class to have caps and gowns.

The Charlotte High School is still on Cooper Street, but attendance has, of course, changed in the years since Buster graduated. With the construction of Lemon Bay High School in Englewood and Port Charlotte High Schools, attendance dropped and then began rising again as new families came and population in the area increased.

Romantic Woes and a Wild Woods Cow

The year 1873 saw the first crude school building; in 1886 the impressive Hotel Punta Gorda was erected and in 1911 a mansion was built on the shores of the Peace River. In its way it was as impressive as the big hotel nearby. The large frame house was in the neighborhood of Retta Esplanade and Sullivan Street. It had five gables and eighteen rooms including a library and music room. A verandah encircled the stately home and the rooms were spacious and airy with tall ceilings and windows overlooking the bay. At high tide, the river could be heard lapping under the house. In those days the shoreline ended at Retta Esplanade.

The owner of this spectacular edifice was Mrs. Martha Susanna Sandlin Morgan; the Sandlin and Morgan families were an integral part of early Trabue and Punta Gorda. I am indebted to Mattie Mae Hughes of our town for the following bit of local history: sometime during the Civil War, Mrs. Mattie Mae Hughes' great-grandfather, Talbert S. Morgan, brought his family here and settled on Cabbage Hammock near the mouth of Alligator Creek. One of his sons, James Martin Morgan, who owned a sawmill on Taylor Road, made a tidy fortune in cattle, shipping and lumber. A partner in the shipping business was James Sandlin who had a trading store in town. The two men fared very well with two boats that plied the Florida west coast carrying lumber, foodstuffs and other goods to the early settlers in the 1880s.

In 1890, James Sandlin built, on Retta Esplanade, the well-known house with the widow's walk that still bears his name. He was a member of the first city council in 1887. James came up the hard way—he was one of three children orphaned at an early age and had to fend for himself in the rough-and-tumble world of frontier days. Once he was established with the successful shipping line, he sent for his sister, Martha Susanna, to join him in Punta Gorda and to marry his partner, James Martin Morgan. It was truly a marriage of convenience, a quite usual occurrence in those times.

James and Martha had six children, four girls and two boys and, as the children grew, all hands learned to work in the family orange grove, another Morgan acquisition. It was in this grove that James Martin Morgan, a rugged individual, finally ran out of luck in 1904. He and his sons, Henry and Jesse, were loading orange crates when there was a sudden shift in the load and one of the large wooden boxes fell on James, the metal stripping gouging through his shin to the bone.

"Typical of my grandfather," says Mattie Mae Hughes, "he didn't do anything about it—just told the boys to finish up he was going hunting. With his leg throbbing painfully, he took his gun, saddled up and rode out to the Big Cypress swamp, trying to take his mind off his critical injury. He rode through stagnant ponds and his horse worked up a good sweat on this feverish hunt. The brackish water combined with the horse's sweat seeping into the open wound brought on an infection. By the time he finally rode back home, his leg was swollen, beet red and was full of fever."

Independent to the end, he dragged himself to the second floor of the house, propped his leg up on a railing of the upstairs porch and bellowed for his daughter to bring him a cup of hot coffee. The next day he swallowed his pride enough to ask to be helped to bed where he died in a matter of hours of blood poisoning.

Martha Susanna Morgan was just as determined an individual as her husband and, after his death, ran the orange grove and tended the cattle with the help of her offspring. She was a firm mother with a lot of native Scottish discipline and kept her children on a short rein.

When her two sons, Henry and Jesse, returned safely from World War I, she expected them to stay at home and work the grove. Henry wasn't much of a worker but Jesse more than made up for that. He was the mainstay of the family and, when he fell in love with a girl named Stella and wanted to get married, Martha Morgan responded with a firm *no*.

Jesse bided his time. One day when his mother was out in the grove working, he hitched up her horse and buggy and headed for his true love, marriage in mind. Somehow, Martha got wind of this and sent two hired hands after her boy with orders to hog-tie him and bring him back.

When Jesse was dragged home, bound hand and foot, he was horse-whipped—another example of his mother's firm discipline. When he recovered physically from this ordeal (he was affected spiritually for the rest of his life) he never went near Stella again. She waited ten years then married someone else. As Mattie Mae puts it, "You might say Grandma ruined Uncle Jesse's life. He had never touched a cigar, cigarette or drunk any whiskey up to that point. Afterward, he just drank, hunted and worked the grove for Grandma. He never married."

Mattie Mae excuses her grandmother by saying that she came here as an immigrant from Scotland with only a few month's schooling. She had been orphaned at an early age, forced into marriage with a man she didn't like and was afraid of losing the son she loved. This son was also vital to her family's livelihood.

This, then, is the lady who spent $50,000 (a fortune in 1911) on a home for her children. She had her own peculiar way of showing love. She not only saw to it that her offspring had a lovely home, but she sent all her daughters to college except for one, Frances Omero, Mattie Mae Hughes' mother whom she kept with her at home.

It was Frances who was the artistic member of the family, who was given music lessons and became a gifted pianist. When her music teacher stated that he had taught her all he could and that she should be sent abroad to study, her mother turned down the suggestion. Thereafter Frances made use of her talents playing for the First Baptist Church that her father and Jim Sandlin had built in town. Life must have palled on a vibrant, talented young girl forced to spend her days taking care of a huge house while her brothers and mother worked the grove and her sisters were away at college.

Romance appeared on the scene with a dashing young man from Fort Myers who swept her off her feet. At the age of fourteen, Frances became a bride and settled down to keeping her own house out on 'Gator Creek, on land her father had willed her. Soon she became pregnant and at the age of fifteen gave birth to a son, James, healthy in all respects save for a malformed foot. Her husband picked this time to leave his child bride and return to Fort Myers, although he visited his wife and infant son on occasion.

When the boy was four, Martha Susanna Morgan paid a New York surgeon $2,000 to come to Punta Gorda and straighten the child's foot. The operation was a success and the father's visits to his son became more frequent. When James was about six, Frances took him to the railroad station to see his daddy off on his return trip to Fort Myers. The little boy clambered up on the train step to hug his father and, as the train pulled out, the father picked up his son and held him close. That was the last Frances saw of her son for eight years. Today the mother would prosecute the father for kidnapping, but not "in the good old days" before women's lib!

This was a traumatic time for the young girl—the ill-fated marriage and abduction of her son—but Frances was a survivor, After a short "vacation" with family, the Preston Sandlins in Jasper, Florida, Frances returned to the family home on Retta Esplanade, immersing herself in keeping the huge house spotless and preparing the meals. She was an excellent cook. In between chores, Frances found solace in playing her beloved piano.

One of the young girl's chores was milking the "woods" cow on the premises. The Morgans didn't own a cow but when Frances' mother spotted a wild cow with calf wandering near the grove, she would set the boys to pen her back of the house. They would feed the cow and keep her for milking.

One of these woods cows was an unusually mean critter with long horns. When Frances put the calf aside and started to milk the mother, the cow charged the girl, pinning her against the fence with her sharp horns. Frances screamed at the top of her lungs, whacking the cow with the milk pail to no avail; the family was all away at the grove.

A young man, new in town, who had just opened a plumbing shop a block away from the Morgan home, heard the frantic screams. Grabbing a heavy pipe, he jumped over the fence—Sir Galahad to the rescue—and beat the cow away from the terrified girl. The young hero's name was Thomas Haywood McDaniel and soon Frances was carrying her delicious pies and cakes to the attractive bachelor. Thomas Haywood had never liked his name and had taken a great deal of kidding over the Haywood name in school, so Frances started calling him Howard and for the rest of his life in Punta Gorda he was known as Howard McDaniel.

Howard was from Tallahassee and as distinctive an individual as either of Frances' own parents: the stubborn, late-departed James Morgan and the strong disciplinarian, Martha Susanna Morgan. He had arrived in Punta Gorda from Bartow where he had worked in the phosphate mines until he had a near-fatal accident. Howard was riding a narrow-gauge railway car when he fell and the bone in one leg was shattered. A doctor was called, took one look and advised amputation. "Never!" said Howard. The doctor shook his head. "If it was only smashed in one place, you might make it, but with two separate breaks, you're going to get gangrene and die." This was before sulfa and penicillin.

Howard persisted in refusing the amputation, the doctor left and a close friend of the injured man took over his care. This buddy brought him food, washed him, took care of his bodily needs, saw to it that he moved as little as possible and kept him well supplied with whiskey. There were no pain pills in those days. Thanks to his stamina and the help of his friend, Howard's leg healed and he was able to walk with only a slight limp.

This finished Howard on the phosphate job and he worked for a while in Perry at a turpentine camp as a guard of the prisoners working there. His reputation as a strong law enforcer led him to Punta Gorda as a deputy sheriff. His stint as a lawman in Punta Gorda was short but the late Judge John T. Rose remembered one incident and told it to Howard's daughter, Mattie Mae McDaniel Hughes, a few years back. "When I was just a little shirt-tailed kid riding my bike around town," the judge told her, "I used to go down to the end of the railroad tracks where there was a saloon. There was a big tree on the bank nearby and we kids would park our bikes up there and sit under the tree watching the saloon because there were fights and all kinds of exciting things might happen. This particular day a jim-dandy fight broke out and someone ran to get your daddy. Pretty soon here comes Mac in his old Model

T. He got out with his gun in his hand and marched into the saloon. Pretty soon here come two men out of that saloon lickety-split, one behind the other with Mac right behind. There was a drainage ditch along the railroad tracks, full of cattails, rushes and debris. Those men jumped into the ditch, sloshing along, running to beat the band, with your daddy standing in the door shooting his gun in the air and shouting 'Don't come back.' Bang. Bang."

Perhaps it was this unorthodox approach to crime that shortened his term as a deputy. Whatever the case, Howard left law enforcement and went into, of all things, the plumbing business, learning the trade under Dave Hobbs. He finally opened his own shop and was there on the fateful day he saved Frances Morgan from the woods cow.

The old adage of "the way to a man's heart is through his stomach" proved true in the case of Howard McDaniel and Frances Morgan. He finally succumbed to a peach cobbler with brandy sauce; wedding bells rang over the loud objections of Martha Susanna Morgan, who had no use for Howard's flamboyant ways and lifestyle. To the day she died, she always referred to him as "*that* McDaniel!"

Chandlers, Tanneries and Penny Candy

When early settler James Madison Lanier lived in his log cabin near the old banyan tree on Retta Esplanade, he traded with the Seminole Indians paddling their canoes around the fat point of land and with the frontier trading post in Hickory Bluff (Charlotte Harbor) across the bay.

After Colonel Isaac Trabue bought Lanier's land, brought the railroad to his little village and instigated the building of the Hotel Punta Gorda, some shops began to sprout up. James Sandlin opened a trading store in Trabue and livery stables and smithies appeared.

In the late 1800s, the Wotitzky family disembarked at the southernmost stop of the Florida Southern Railroad. Jacob Wotitzky opened a general merchandise store on Marion Avenue which carried a little bit of everything. He was so successful that later on his son, Edward, extended the business to outlying islands, sailing his boat as far south as the Ten Thousand Islands and the Florida Keys, selling supplies to the isolated early settlers.

The Hart family of Philadelphia had arrived at about the same time and owned a ships chandlery on Retta Esplanade at Cross Street. Gus and Dora Hart served local fishing boats and even ocean-going freighters, merchandise being trundled by oxcart down a lane to the water's edge and loaded onto the waiting ships. The store burned in 1896 and, unnerved by this disaster, the family returned to their native Philadelphia and their former life there. However, their daughter, Celia, later returned to Punta Gorda as a young lady to visit an aunt and met Edward Wotitzky. Edward and Celia became the parents of the prominent attorneys in town, Frank and Leo Wotitzky.

At the turn of the century, before river silt was pumped in to create Laishley Park and the mobile home area (now the Harbor Walk development at Laishley Park), the Peace River shore reached East Retta Esplanade. There was a ships chandlery, owned and operated by Flusser Manning Glover, where the Dean's South of The Border Restaurant now stands. Glover had come here in the early 1900s from Norfolk, Virginia, as an engineer on the boats, met Jessie Mae Lile, who was visiting the I. W. Johnsons of Punta Gorda, and fell in love.

That was the end of Flusser's bachelorhood and he settled happily into married life. Leaving the boats, he opened a ships chandlery next door to Johnny Brown's Machine Shop and Johnny Sand's Boat Yard.

The rest of the surrounding land along the shore was used for boat storage, large tarpaulins protecting them from the weather. The waters of the Peace River lapped against the backyards of these establishments.

Soon the Glovers became a family with the arrival of a daughter, Mary Ellen. The ships chandlery business was good and it was a pleasant life for them. Mary Ellen Glover (Manning) remembers playing hide-and-seek among the stored boats with her best friend, Wanda Bassett. The Bassett home was a two-story house built high off the ground (because possible flooding) near the Glover store across from the big hotel.

A narrow-gauge railway ran parallel to the main line from the ice house on Virginia down to the waterfront dock. An ice-car powered by a gasoline engine carried the ice to the fish companies on the waterfront and sometimes the two little girls would hitch a ride to Wanda's house or the Glover store on these cars. It was dangerous fun, but saved them a lot of walking.

Mary Ellen remembers there was one area on Marion Avenue that the two girls particularly avoided when they were walking. Mr. Kinsel had a small tannery where he cured alligator hides and made them into pocketbooks, shoes and belts. The odor of formaldehyde was overpowering to anyone walking down that part of the street.

Just as Mary Ellen was nearing her teens, Flusser Glover built a large home in Cleveland and moved his family there. Although the young girl still attended school in Punta Gorda, her social life changed.

It was a longer and more arduous trip now to the Seminole pharmacy for ice cream and for a visit to her good friend, Wanda Bassett. The Cleveland house was very spacious and friends would visit. The days of hitchhiking on the ice cars, playing in the boatyard and crabbing in the bay were a thing of the past.

After graduating from high school in 1932, Mary Ellen left for a protracted visit with her father's family in Virginia where she met a good-looking young man, Joseph Manning, and in 1934 Mary Ellen and Joe were married. After Flusser Glover's death, Joe took over the reins of the Glover Ships Chandlery and built a hardware store on Marion Avenue. When all the chandlery's inventory was moved to the new location and the old establishment closed, Manning's Hardware store took its place.

In the early 1900s there was a sprawling eight-bedroom house on the bayfront in Charlotte Harbor. In this house lived Harry and Bertha Gaskill and their seven children. Harry was a commercial fisherman and a fishing guide on Useppa Island. The Gaskill home was full of activity from sunup to sundown. You can imagine the bedlam with seven kids under one roof! The oldest boy, Anson, one of twins, was born in this house in 1912.

A neighbor of the Gaskills, Mott Willis, owned the only store in Charlotte Harbor. "It was a country store, little bit of everything: medicine, yard goods, pickles hardware, groceries."

Mott's son, Carl, made one delivery a week, usually on Saturday with horse and wagon. Dexter, the horse, was approaching senility and spooked very easily. One Saturday, little Anson, trudging along the dirt road by Willis's store, saw Dexter hitched up to the fully loaded wagon and dozing in the sun. Anson also noticed a cat loping through the tall weeds by the side of the road. "I'll never know what got into me, but I picked up that cat and plunked him down on Dexter's back."

The terrified cat dug in his claws and poor old Dexter, rudely awakened from his nap, careened off toward the horizon. Bread, eggs, fruit, and flour flew through the air and the wagon soon became kindling wood. "I never said anything about it, kept it to myself, because I would have been in a peck of trouble!"

Dexter recovered.

The country store wasn't Mott Willis' only source of income. He ran the mail boat back and forth from Punta Gorda to Charlotte Harbor and also carried passengers. During the hunting season, Mott always carried a gun on the crossing and passengers were quite accustomed to stopping along the way while Mott took aim at ducks overhead. People weren't in such a rush in those days and there was time to stop and smell the roses—or, in this case, bag the birds.

In 1901, Dr. David Norman McQueen hung out his shingle in Old Punta Gorda, becoming one of the town's first doctors. In addition to his regular practice and position as a state inspector, the doctor also owned a twenty-five-acre citrus grove on Shell Creek and a thirty-acre vegetable farm across from where Banyan Point is now. As if this weren't enough to keep him busy, he bought a building that Ed Smith had just erected on Marion Avenue and Taylor Street and he started the Seminole Pharmacy. Hugh Mobley had just gotten his sheepskin from the University of Mississippi's School of Pharmacy and Dr. McQueen hired him as his pharmacist. The Seminole Pharmacy was the first drugstore and soda fountain in Charlotte County. Later, the good doctor sold the drugstore to Wallace Mobley and it became a popular meeting place for young and old. "Let's go to Mobleys for a banana split."

Faye Mobley Austin, daughter of "Doc" and Elsie Whitehurst, remembers that while she and her young friends were swimming in the bay on hot, dusty afternoons, "The ladies would get all dressed up, saunter down to the post office, check their mail and walk to Mobley's Seminole Pharmacy for a cherry smash—it was a ritual."

Martha Weeks McCormack, a daughter of Matt and Mamie Weeks (Weeks Machine Shop and Boat Works) reminisces: "Mobley's had nickel ice cream cones, two large dips. We kids really enjoyed those!" Jane Weeks Watson and brother, Wayne Weeks, remember another store youngsters enjoyed, McClelland's candy store. "Mr. McClelland had a store in front of his funeral home and you could get a bag of penny candy you wouldn't believe!"

Tosie Hindman, daughter of Cap'n Fred and Belle Quednau, has still a different recollection of McClelland's. "We used to have scavenger hunts when I was a kid and McClelland's Funeral Parlor was a prime target. It was in an isolated part of town and 'spooky.' If you could grab something from there, a doormat or anything, you were a candidate for first prize. We never broke a thing and always returned what we took."

Another favorite place in town was Maxwell's Pharmacy. Mary Furman (Maxwell) was born in Birmingham, Alabama, on December 13, 1901. Her parents, Theodore and Harriet Furman already had five other children, nevertheless Mary was a welcome Christmas present. Her father "was in an old-fashioned business—he was a tailor. He ran his own shop, taking his customers' measurements and drawing up his own patterns." Mary is a direct descendent of Richard Furman who, in 1826, founded Furman University in Greenville, South Carolina.

From her early years, little Mary showed an unusual interest in music and was gifted with a lovely voice. In her teens, she sang for local groups, at weddings, hotel functions and for the Birmingham Junior Music Club. She might have had a singing career but, at the age of eleven, her school deskmate introduced her to a dashing young man of nineteen, Roscoe "Mack" Maxwell.

Mary was just a child when they met, but after Mack's return from his service with the Medical Corps in World War I, he found the little girl had grown into a lovely young woman. In 1920 Mack and Mary were married in Birmingham. The young bride wore her great great-grandmother's "second day" wedding dress.

In olden times the bride usually wore a dress of subdued color on her wedding day. On the day after the wedding, the "second day" there was much celebrating with parties and a formal ball. "Most newly-weds didn't go on a wedding trip or honeymoon in those days; traveling was so difficult."

On the festive "second day," the bride wore a more elaborate and colorful dress, the "second day" dress. Her great great-grandmother's gown was exquisite, made of silver cloth with embroidered maize bouquets on it. Mary still treasures it.

The young couple settled in Birmingham where Mack was the pharmacist for a local drug store. Soon a baby boy arrived, Roscoe Steele Maxwell Jr. The little boy was never called Junior but went through life as "Rocky" and later became the beloved Dr. Rocky Maxwell of the Medical Center Hospital (Charlotte Regional Medical Center).

By 1923 Mary and Mack Maxwell with their newborn son, Rocky, had settled into a busy life in the bustling metropolis of Birmingham, Alabama. The young pharmacist worked for a well-established drug store and, though little Rocky kept her close to home, Mary still found time to sing with the Birmingham Junior Music Club and at other social events.

Everything was going smoothly when a letter arrived from Mack's brother, Finklea, who lived in Punta Gorda. He extolled the virtues of the little town and urged his brother to move to this growing community. Being an adventurous young man, Mack made the decision to take the big step and moved his little family to this new promising location.

On May Day, 1926 the Maxwells arrived in Punta Gorda. Construction was booming; workmen were busy hammering and sawing, putting the finishing touches on the town's new Arcade. Mack decided this was the perfect location for his drug store and, when the Arcade was finished, Maxwell's Pharmacy opened its doors.

It was a handsome emporium. In those days a drugstore was not only a pharmacy but also an ice cream parlor. Mack had spared nothing on the furnishings: there were limed oak triangular chairs to slip under the matching circular tables with milk glass tops. The marble counter was long and backed by a sparkling mirror. The fountain was outfitted with numerous gadgets to make sodas, concoct elaborate sundaes or the popular banana split. An impressive display of gleaming glassware lined the shelves. The entrance doors folded back so that the entire store was completely open—an innovation in those days.

Also, way back then, it became a social custom to await the arrival of the evening mail train at Maxwell's Pharmacy, sipping a cherry smash or eating a dish of ice cream while waiting for the mail to be sorted. Before the evening mail train arrived at the depot, every table and chair in Maxwell's Pharmacy was occupied and the young local "fountain boys" were swamped with orders.

Looking back on the stores of that time, Mary Maxwell remembers in particular the Seward's store on Marion Avenue. Kirby Seward had been founder and publisher of the *Punta Gorda Herald* until 1901 when Adrian Jordan took over the reins. Kirby's wife, Laura, was Ed

Wotitzky's sister, and she presided over the Emporium. The main floor was filled with racks of dresses, but there were also drygoods, bolts of lace, shelves of high-button shoes and more. A balcony in the back of the store displayed more intimate apparel, corsets of appalling rigidity, ladies' drawers of more than ample proportions and corset covers to hide the unattractive metal stays.

Mary remembers that Miss Laura, as everyone called her, was always elegantly groomed with a large diamond pin on the front of her dress. Her best friend was Mrs. Norman Hewitt, "Miss Frankie." She, Miss Laura and Mrs. Hancock were very prominent ladies in town.

Another shop was run by a Mr. Smith, a Spanish gentleman, and his English wife, Melody. This establishment had a smattering of everything from dishpans to needles and thread. Elmer Oswald, Miss Esther's brother, had a men's clothing store. There was a Charlotte Drugstore, King's Furniture Store, and a grocery store in the Arcade run by Byron Rhode. There was Peeples' IGA store, and Griggs' Groceteria where you had to order your lettuce ahead of time!

Doc McQueen recalls other stores such as Jim Goff's garage where "I can remember my dad writing out a check for $150 for a new body for his Model T." Young McQueen was a worker and held many jobs in his early teens. He drove a dairy truck for Howard Dreggers and the Brown Dairy. "I loaded the truck around five A.M., then I and the night watchman at the big hotel would take a dip in the hotel pool. After our swim he'd go home to sleep and I'd hop in the truck and start making deliveries."

Doc also worked for Blount's Grocery Store. He was bag boy, swept up and made deliveries, this for twenty-five cents an afternoon. "I had a twenty-inch bike. Mr. Blount made a basket for it out of a box that corned beef came in and I'd deliver loaves of bread, a dozen eggs, packages of cheese, little items like that—all the basket would hold. Later on I graduated to a dollar on Saturday—seven in the morning 'til nine at night. The first Saturday I was paid a dollar, I went to Seward's Drygoods Store and bought me a pair of overalls for a dollar!"

* * *

When Byron Leslie Rhode was just a small tot, his father, George, pulled up stakes and moved the household to Sullivan Street in Punta

Gorda. He remembers the town of those days as "just a little village." King Street was a railroad right of way for the trains approaching the depot, which was situated approximately two blocks south of the Barron Collier Bridge and across U.S. 41 from where the Punta Gorda Mall is today. Trains from the north backed into the station while those from the south headed in and then backed out. Byron remembers Cleve and Jean Cleveland's wedding, when Gilchrist ran for governor, when Vernon Peeples, our former state representative, was just a little shaver and Tosie Hindman's mother, Belle Quednau was "the prettiest girl in town."

Byron's father, George Rhode, was a partner in Fortson and Rhode, a combination ships chandlery and grocery store in the Dade Hotel (later, The Seminole). This business venture was not a success and shut up shop in 1910. George turned to farming for a while and then became postmaster of Punta Gorda from 1912 to 1921. George was an invalid during the last years of his life, and to make ends meet, his wife, Docia, opened a boarding house located on the corner of Goldstein and Marion streets, across from city hall.

Byron, who now had three sisters, cut cordwood after school to help with the family finances. When his father died, Byron quit school and went to work in the sawmills. Later he became a commercial fisherman. By 1928 Byron was engineer on a freight/passenger boat, *The Harris Brothers*, running out of Punta Gorda. One of its stops was Bokeelia where a pretty girl, Alice Blanche Riddle, caught his eye. She wouldn't change her name until he "got off that boat!" It was an easy choice to make.

At this time, the Bever brothers owned a chain of B&B grocery stores all over Florida. The new bridegroom guaranteed the brothers $1,000 a week gross in Punta Gorda, if they'd open a store. On December 6, 1928, Byron opened the fifth B&B store which later became U-Save. After a falling out with the Bevers, he left to open a Home Supply Store in the Arcade across from Maxwell's Pharmacy.

After many years, Byron Rhode and his wife moved to Jacksonville. However, Byron continued to visit Punta Gorda, making a special visit for the Centennial's Old Timers' Day. What a wealth of memories this "hometown boy" had stored away!

In 1876 when Alfred Gilbert Barnhill arrived in Pine Level, James Lanier was still in Fort Ogden. It would be another five years before he made his trek to the south shores of the Peace River on land later purchased by Colonel Trabue.

Alfred Barnhill planted a large citrus grove on his Pine Level homestead, the oldest grove with the largest trees in this part of the state. He also was instrumental in establishing the first school in the area.

Alfred had a son, Eveleth, who married Frances Denty and they had an only child, Leroy. In 1911, when Leroy was three, Eveleth moved his little family to Boca Grande where they lived at Mrs. Tillis' boarding house.

Eveleth opened a country store and Leroy remembers that, by the door, there was a keg of sweet apple cider with a community tin cup. In the summer folks would come from the other islands with live chickens to swap for groceries. The chickens were kept in a pen, and come winter and tourists, the birds would reappear as dressed poultry in the meat case.

There were many wealthy families on Gasparilla Island, such as the DuPonts and Vanderbilts. They had come to the island for peace and quiet and saw to it that automobiles were banned in their southern retreat.

The sole vehicle allowed to operate on the island was a Model T that carried elderly guests from the Gasparilla Inn to the nearby golf course. Eveleth grasped this opportunity to open a dray business, carrying the bulky steamer trunks of the day, horse-drawn wagon loads of them, from the depot to the hotels. Besides the Gasparilla Inn, there were two other hotels operated by a Mr. Howell.

Eveleth also helped build roads on the island and was, obviously, a very busy man. Little Leroy, now motherless, was taken care of by Mrs. Tillis, her daughters and a maid.

When Leroy was thirteen, his father moved them back to Punta Gorda. Robert Harris had bought the old Marshall place on Alligator Creek and Leroy's father supervised the building of the Allapatchee Lodge out there.

The boy attended Charlotte High School and after classes helped his dad "clean up" the land around the lodge and build a road to it.

Always industrious like his father, Leroy also worked after school at Grigg's grocery.

Sallie Jones' brothers had a meat market next door and business was good until the A&P moved into Punta Gorda. With Grigg's business tapering off, Leroy went to work for the B&B and after about a year was made manager.

In World War II, Leroy fought with distinction with the 85th Infantry Division in Africa and Italy, winning three combat ribbons and the Bronze Star. His job as manager of the B & B was waiting for him after the war. He met his future wife, Dallas Roper, when she was working at the PX at the airfield and they were married in 1957.

Leroy retired from the B&B in 1967. He saw the A&P close its doors, unable to compete with the B&B, Winn-Dixie and Publix, just as the small grocers had been unable to compete with the A&P.

The original IGA store in Punta Gorda was run by Mr. Griggs and upon his death a young enterprising Floridian couple, Vasco and Lois Cole Peeples, bought the business. The first location was on West Marion Avenue one block east of Cross Street. Later it was moved to its final spot on the corner of Marion Avenue and Cross Street. Lois Cole Peeples' family history is a unique one and gives us an insight into the fortitude and ingenuity of our early settlers.

In the early 1900s young Gus and Abbie Cole were among the handful of settlers on little Tidy Island in Sarasota Bay. Gus was a commercial fisherman and when their baby girl, Lois, was born, he moved his little family south to Gasparilla Island where access to the Gulf made fishing even better.

When Lois was less than a year old, the Coles packed all their belongings on a sailboat and set forth on this new adventure. A short stay on the island proved that Gus's hunch was correct; fish were abundant in this island chain. On the strength of this, the young fisherman bought a small island from the state and settled his family there. This little spot of land in Gasparilla Bay is known to this day as Cole Island. You come upon it immediately after paying the toll on the bridge to Boca Grande.

As his daughter was approaching school age, Gus began to worry about her education. He himself had never gone beyond the second grade and this fact made him determined that his children would have proper schooling.

Lois didn't go to school until her next two brothers "reached learning age"; then Gus found a certified teacher on Gasparilla Island and "paid her so much apiece to teach us." Lois, Ralph and Bert took a rowboat to the teacher's house on the main island for their lessons. They would row home in the afternoon with Abbie or Gus keeping a weather eye out for their return. Later a public school was formed and the children attended it.

The family was growing and finally there were seven children in all—two boys and five girls. With that awesome number of mouths to feed, Gus supplemented his income as a commercial fisherman by also acting as a fishing guide. Among the people he took out were a family from Lima, Ohio, owners of the Lima Tea Company in that city. Impressed with Gus they offered him a job as shipping clerk. Always ready for a new challenge and opportunity, Gus accepted. Life up north was not only drastically different for the Coles, but it was too cold! One winter was enough for Gus, Abbie and the children. "Papa decided he didn't want to live in any northern state, the weather was just too chilly. When we came back home in 1918, our furniture was delayed due to the war so we went to a little place Papa had on what was then called Little Gasparilla. When the furniture came, we moved to Boca Grande."

The Cole's stay in Boca Grande was relatively short, "only about a school year," and not too sweet. There was a typhoid fever epidemic and some of the Cole children contracted the disease. The doctor had to come from Arcadia by train. He'd arrive in the morning, spend the day with patients and return to Arcadia by the afternoon train. Everyone in the family recovered and returned to school. Lois remembers the principal of that school was U. S. Whiteaker, U. S. Cleveland's grandfather.

A freak accident in the little town of Gasparilla on the northern end of the island drastically changed the Coles' lifestyle. A Mr. O. J. Vickers owned the fish house and ran a general merchandise store in the small town. In the year 1919 he had a fatal encounter with a stinger (stingray). He was stung, developed blood poisoning and died. Mr. Vicker's tragedy was Gus Cole's good fortune. Gus was soon owner of the store and postmaster of the little post office.

The Coles moved into the Vickers' rambling, one-story, frame house "built on posts seven or eight feet high to avoid high water. We had to climb a flight of steps to get to the porch." There was enough room so that, even with seven children underfoot, the home did not bulge at the seams. Lois' mother, Abbie, had her hands full seeing to it that her large brood was clothed and fed. Lois remembers her mother had "a wash day, an ironing day and several baking days." There didn't seem to be enough days in the week for Abbie Cole!

The children went to a one-room schoolhouse that was close enough so they could come home for lunch. "Our favorite meal was fish, lima beans and cornbread. When we knew Mama was cooking that, we couldn't get home fast enough." The family's diet did not include much meat, but "we really celebrated when we had turtle meat. Mama ground it up (turtleburgers) or made it into a delicious stew." Turtle eggs were not overlooked either, Abbie used them in making her cakes—fifty eggs to a cake! There was always plenty of sea grape and guava jelly in the cupboard, bounty from the land.

"We drank canned milk. Papa, of course, had the general store and bought it by the case. There were no cows on the island. We had an icebox with a drip pan and got our ice from the fish house. We didn't really need refrigeration with nine in the family. We ate everything on our plates and Mama cooked every day. When kerosene refrigerators came into being, Papa bought one; that's when we thought we were really doing well. We used kerosene lamps to read by and, when the new Aladdin lamps took their place, we had one. Our Aladdin was a prized possession and we kept it on display in the living room.

"Papa liked music, he used to play a guitar when he was a fisherman. He always wanted music in the house and we had a phonograph with a large horn. The music was on round cylinders you inserted into the machine. My favorite was 'Over the Waves.'

"Papa's store carried hardware, groceries, dry goods, shoes— everything that was normally used by commercial fishermen. If they needed anything more than that, there was always the Sears Roebuck catalogue."

Gus Cole was self-educated, having had no schooling past the second grade. This didn't stop him, though. Working in a grocery store at age eleven to help his widowed mother "he learned to add and subtract by working at problems like a puzzle. He'd get some customer to make up math problems and he'd work them out, using grocery bags as scrap paper. He'd work at them until he got them right. That was why Papa was such a stickler about us getting an education."

Abbie made all the children's clothes but never bought a pattern. When she saw something she liked in a paper or a magazine, she'd cut her own pattern. Lois recalls laughingly that, when her mother shopped in her husband's store, she often brought home a large bolt of cloth and made girls' dresses and boys' shirts alike from it. Brothers and sisters went to school wearing the same material, the same color and print.

If Gus Cole had been a millionaire, he would most certainly have been a philanthropist. At Christmas time, his chief concern was that every child in the town of Gasparilla should have presents from Santa. He saw to it that there was a towering tree decked with all the trimmings in the schoolhouse, which doubled as the church. There was a yuletide program with candy, fruit and gifts for all. This holiday party was the high point of the season for the local families.

Gus was also concerned about the local fishermen who had a hard time making ends meet, especially in times of sickness and death. He did something about it. Gus sold gasoline to the fishermen and he added one cent per gallon to the price, putting the extra money in a special fund for them. He made a permanent arrangement with a mortician in Arcadia for the funerals and burials of the local people. When a fisherman died, Gus called the mortuary and they shipped him a casket at the prearranged price. This foresightedness saved the widow and family from financial problems at a time of grief.

Naturally, there were no facilities for embalming on the island so the family and friends sat up all night, as in the old Irish wakes; to comfort the bereaved and to make sure the lately departed was finally at peace! The next day a boatacade sailed forth to Englewood, the burial place, with the leading boat carrying the casket, other boats following. Upon arrival at the Englewood shore, the funeral party tramped through palmettos and wild growth to the cemetery where a layman conducted the services. This whole procedure was made easier by Gus' thoughtful creation of the seamen's fund.

Lois's mother, Abbie, had grandparents who were getting up in years and came to live in a little cottage behind the Coles' rambling house. They were Narsisco and Concepcione de Noda. Narsisco had been a sea captain and had come to Palma Sola (near Bradenton) from Spain by way of the Canary Islands and Cuba. He had met his wife on one of his stopovers in Key West where she was a schoolteacher. The handsome old couple had privacy in their own small home in Gasparilla. There was a walkway from their cottage to the back of the big house where they could stroll in at will, then leave when the clamor of seven children became too much for them.

The ninety-seven-year-old sea captain didn't actually retire when he and his wife came to live with their granddaughter and great-grandchildren on Gasparilla Island. Narsisco kept himself busy stoking Abbie's pressing iron with coal on ironing day, cutting wood to burn under her outdoor washpot and making soap for her laundry. He made the soap from lye and fat or grease, letting it harden and then cutting it into bars. He claimed soap had to be made when the moon was in a certain phase or it would not harden.

Lois most fondly remembers her great grandfather. "When he was about 100 years old, we missed him one day—finally found him cutting mangroves back in the woods for Mama's washpot. He is buried up on Englewood and died of natural causes when he was 102 or so. He was active right up until the end, with no physical problems—he just plain wore out."

By this time, Lois had finished eighth grade and, in keeping with Gus's insistence on education, moved to Tampa where she lived with an aunt and attended Tampa Business College. A young man named Vasco Peeples had been teaching her brothers and sisters until he moved to a new position in the Vineland School. However, he still went back to Gasparilla to visit the Coles, particularly when he knew Lois would be home on a visit. "All my brothers and sisters liked Vasco very much."

When Lois finished college she worked with Gus in the store and saw Vasco Peeples on occasion. "There wasn't much to do when boys came to see girls in Gasparilla. We just visited more or less." These visits became more and more often and finally there was to be a wedding.

August 14, 1926, dawned overcast and gloomy on Gasparilla Island, but in the Cole home all was gaiety and excitement. The former principal of the Cole children's school on the island was marrying their sister, Lois. That dreary morning the young bride-to-be worried as she walked to her father's store on her last day of work. It looked as if a terrible storm was brewing and "Vasco had to walk that long trestle from Placida and I thought, *my goodness, he'll never get over here.*"

But Vasco was persistent. He drove with a justice of the peace beside him, over the slippery dirt road from Englewood to Placida in a blinding storm. Then, leaving the car at Placida, the men had to navigate on foot the two miles of railroad trestle to Gasparilla and the anxious bride-to-be. The ceremony took place on time in the Cole living room and, after the festivities were over, one of Lois' brothers took the newlyweds back to the mainland in his boat—a memorable wedding day!

After their honeymoon, the young couple embarked on a scholastic odyssey ending in Tallahassee. In 1927, both newlyweds taught school in O'Brien, and later that same year Vasco attended summer school at the University of Florida. It was there, in Gainesville, that the first child, Carmen Catherine, was born. Late in 1927 Vasco became principal of the school in McAlpine, and in early 1928 they both taught at Tiger Lake, all in Suwannee County. That year they moved to Live Oak, where he was elected state representative from Suwannee County. He served in the state legislature in Tallahassee in 1929 while Lois worked in a secretarial pool there. During this busy time, Vasco's mother minded baby Carmen.

The following year saw the young couple returned to Live Oak and in 1930 a son, Vernon, was born. This same year Vasco opened a meat market (later an IGA grocery store) in Live Oak and it prospered for three years. He moved his family to Punta Gorda in 1933 at the urging of his father-in-law, who had one of the first IGA stores in Florida and knew of an opening in Punta Gorda. Lois's father had become a very successful business man, postmaster of Gasparilla and Placida and wanted the little family closer to him, just across the harbor.

Vasco's original store on Marion Avenue was just two blocks west of the Tamiami Trail. It was a grocery store and meat market and delivered "even a single loaf of bread." Deliveries were made by boys on bicycles and among some of the young boys who clerked and generally "helped out" were Frank Smoak, Doc Whitehurst, Leonard Wetherington and Joe Addison.

Doc Whitehurst remembers the day he started working at Peeples IGA "as soon as I could reach the second shelf in the store. I delivered groceries on a bicycle and I worked in the store, doing a little bit of everything. Lois Peeples is the hardest working woman I've ever known. They were hard up then, Vasco and Lois, they had to dig to make a living in those days. They scratched in that store to make ends meet, trying to compete with the A&P and the B&B, but they gave credit to any family that needed it. They ran their business mainly on credit and therefore they never had much cash on hand, but had hundreds of friends. Maybe a shipment of groceries would come in, might not be more than $80. Lois would go upstairs and Vasco would go down the street; they would dig to get that $80 in cash. Many of the old customers charged their groceries and were very slow in paying but Vasco and Lois never refused credit. What I'm trying to say is that Vasco and Lois finally did prosper, but they deserved to prosper. They were so good to so many people."

Travis Parnell, later sheriff, was one of the butchers and Jack Koon used to distribute handbills for the store. Lois would drive the car "with Jack on the running board. I'd just keep driving and Jack would hop off and on again delivering pamphlets about the weekend IGA specials."

By the year 1935 the Peeples' store was doing so well that Vasco and Lois decided to leave their rented building on Marion and buy one a block west on the corner of Marion and Cross. The young family moved their inventory to the new location and settled themselves in comfortable living quarters above the store.

The transition was made in the fall of 1935 and the following year little Gussie Peeples was born in their new home. Her first playpen was a large cardboard box in the store where Lois and the customers could keep an eye on her. This tradition of family togetherness continued with the presence of great-grandson Bryan's crib in Lois's office in the Peeples Agency, Inc. Abbie Cole's daughter has followed her mother's example of hard work, busy days and love of family.

In 1938 Lois Zoel Peeples was born, like her sister, in the family home above the IGA store. Now the family was complete. Lois Sr. kept the homefires burning, assisted Vasco in the store and kept active in church work and civic affairs.

During World War II, she became head of the family and operated the store while Vasco served with the U.S. Army Corps of Engineers in Brazil and the Azores. These were rough times for Lois, coping with customers and their ration books, learning how to butcher meat, tending to the bookkeeping and raising a family.

Young Tosie Hindman, a family friend, helped Lois in the store and became her sometime butcher; the older children, Carmen and Vernon, were barely in their teens, but did all they could to help out. Tosie chuckles as she recalls, "Neither of us knew how to cut meat, so Travis Parnell, then deputy sheriff, came over at night and showed us how to break down a quarter of beef, cut up beef liver, grind hamburger, etc."

Gussie Peeples Baker was just a little girl then, but she remembers, "Mother always gave our ration stamps away—someone always needed them more than we did." Gussie also recalls the park across from the store (Hessler's Carpets is there now). There was an octagonal bandstand there and beside it stood a huge barbed-wire container to hold Punta Gorda's contribution to the war effort in the way of scrap metal and paper. At the war's end Vasco returned to take over the reins again. In addition to the IGA, he also opened a Firestone store he had franchised and a small automobile agency for Hudsons, Willys and Crosleys.

Vasco's next venture was in land development. He soon became aware that the retirees, coming in droves to Florida and with a newly found leisure time on their hands, fully expected to have golf courses awaiting them. In its heyday the Hotel Charlotte Harbor had a course east of town, but it had long since been abandoned. Vasco, with the help of many local people—Leo Wotitzky, Drayton Farr, Milton Davis, Ralph Phelps, Joyce Hindman and Agnes Craighead among them— acquired the property and began the arduous clean-up program.

Trees were felled, the jungle of weeds rooted out and a golf course began to take shape. Today the Punta Gorda Country Club is a thriving eighteen-hole golf course and the original club building stood until it burned and a new building took its place.

In 1952 a polio epidemic struck in the little town of Punta Gorda. Three died, and one of the victims was fourteen-year-old Lois Zoel Peeples. In their grief Vasco and Lois kept themselves busy with their many interests but sold the IGA store and built a home on Aqui Esta away from constant memories of their youngest child.

Vasco by now had developed Aqui Esta, Alta Vista, off Taylor Road, and Rio Villa on Alligator Creek and the Punta Gorda Kampgrounds. He also found time to be chairman of the county commissioners. His last project was the golf course near Windmill Village. Vasco died April 20, 1985 and his son, Vernon, delivered the eulogy. Lois remarks, "We worked together when we taught school, we worked together in the grocery store and in the office; we had worked together ever since we were married. We would have been married sixty-one years in August of 1987 if he had lived."

Lois has always been a person in her own right, though. Her accomplishments are staggering: twice president of the Women's Club, president of the Business and Professional Women's Club, president of the Charlotte County Democratic Women's Club, Woman of the year 1957, historian for the Red Cross, Women's Club and Democratic Women's Club of Florida.

The Peeples family has contributed an amazingly rich legacy to our town: Vasco and Lois with all their activities, Vernon, state representative and Gussie Peeples Baker, general chairman of the Punta Gorda Area Centennial Committee and new Peeples are still coming!

* * *

When the Jones family moved to Punta Gorda in 1901, from Bartow, it was not the happiest of times for them. Josie Jones' husband, Charles, Marshal of Bartow, had just died from malaria at the age of thirty-eight and the young widow had come to town with her four children to be near her brother, Luther Koon. Luther, a prosperous cattleman, helped his sister as best he could and the plucky young widow sewed for the local women and also worked as a practical nurse. Her oldest son, Neal, quit school at the age of nine to work in his uncle's slaughter house to help support the family.

Years of hard work earned the family success in our little town; the lone girl, Sallie, grew up to become the beloved teacher for whom the Sallie Jones Elementary School is named and her three brothers, Neal, Charlie and Ferg owned and operated the thriving Jones Brothers Meat Market on Marion Avenue.

Areta Yeager Futch, in looking back upon her childhood in Punta Gorda remembers the Jones Brothers Meat Market most fondly. When she was a little girl, her mother often sent her there with an order. The tiny girl would stand quietly on the sawdust floor, waiting to be served and with a wistful eye on one of her favorite foods in the meat case. After filling her mother's order, Charlie Jones would hesitate for a moment, then say, "Little Areta, I have something for you," reach into the case and hand her a hot dog. The young girl would skip happily home with the order, munching the cold frankfurter on the way. "I learned to eat it before I got home, because Mother would have a fit if she knew I ate it uncooked." Areta still loves hot dogs, but she doesn't eat them raw anymore!

One of the last of the small grocery stores in town was Lawhorne's Food Palace. John T. "Dick" Lawhorne came to town in 1941 from Arcadia and bought the building on the corner of Marion and Taylor.

From 1906 to 1913 the *Punta Gorda Herald* published its newspaper upstairs in the rear of the building; the telephone company was located in the second-floor front. The *Herald* was forced to move because, when the presses were rolling they shook the entire building! Until the time that Dick Lawhorne opened his grocery, there had been a hardware store downstairs.

Nancy Lawhorne Raulerson was two when she came here with her parents, Dick and Elizabeth. The oldest of four children, she remembers the excitement of those Saturday nights when everybody came to town. "The streets were full of people milling around—just like the Annual Block Party." When she was older, she used to drive with her daddy in his truck out to the Maud Street dock (now Fishermen's Village) to deliver groceries to the fish houses. The fishermen would need supplies before setting out on their weekly runs down the harbor.

Nancy remembers that once, when she was a toddler, she climbed the backstairs of the grocery store to visit with the friendly telephone operators. She also recalls watching her parents use the big old wall phone, waiting for the "number please" before they could place their call.

Dick Lawhorne became clerk of the circuit court in 1956, closing his grocery store and leasing the building to Abstract Title and later to attorney John Hathaway. Nancy sold the property in 1984.

* * *

The fishing of the early frontiersmen in the late 1800s for food and provender had grown into a booming industry with the arrival of the railroad into little Trabue in 1886. Fish now could be shipped in ice to northern consumers and another business emerged from all this—the ice business. The ice house was located on Virginia Avenue and had a narrow gauge railway running from the plant to the fish companies on the waterfront. "Ice cars" powered by gasoline engines operated on this miniature railroad, carrying their valuable cargo to the dock, to the fish houses and the waiting railroad cars.

Later, the fish houses were removed to the Maud Street dock and the narrow-gauge track was torn up. The ice house continued in business. In the 1920s there were no refrigerators, only ice boxes awaiting the iceman's delivery of the twenty-five and fifty-pound blocks of ice. One such delivery man was Sherrod Smith, affectionately known around town as "the Smiling Iceman." It was not that the other iceman was an unpleasant fellow; it was just that Sherrod always had a smile on his face, even after carrying a fifty-pound block of ice up a long flight of stairs, only to be told, "Sorry, no ice today." "All right, see you tomorrow," he'd say, still with a grin on his face.

Sherrod Smith was a North Carolina farmer who came to Punta Gorda when many of his family migrated to Florida in the 1920s. In Punta Gorda, he and his wife, Ethel, found an ideal house in which to live. They rented the upstairs of Fred and Belle Quednau's home on Marion Avenue and immediately became part of the friendly Quednau family. In 1930, when Ethel gave birth at home to her daughter, Edna Earl, Dr. Blount attended. Although her mother was the oldest of thirteen children, Edna Earl was to be the Smiths' only child.

Soon Edna Earl was old enough to crawl to the top of the stairs (protected by a gate) and plead, "Wanna come down, Aunt B.? Wanna come down." Tosie—Fred and Belle's daughter—"used to play with me like I was one of her dolls, pushing me wildly around in my carriage." The Smiths lived for "seven years and seven months with Aunt Belle and Uncle Fred, then we moved down just a block. Our house faced Dolly Street and is still standing.

"Sherrod's ice truck had a metal body with a crossbar in the middle to keep the ice from sliding to the back and there was also a tarpaulin to keep it from melting. Jeanette Whitehorse, her sister Faye and Eloise Adams would get in the bed of the truck, hide behind that canvas and ride for blocks before daddy realized they were there. He never made them walk home, but always carried them back.

"I used to go with daddy every chance I got; I particularly liked to go up there to the ice house. The ice was stored in vats on the floor and there was a big overhead boom to lift the huge blocks of ice. There were two hooks on the boom and I would put my foot in one and ride across; it was fun and exciting." Edna Earl drove around town with her father making deliveries and "there was one thing I dearly looked forward to; I always got a hamburger at the Orange Grille, one block down from the ice house."

The ice business was good and Sherrod was a busy man. He even delivered as far as El Jobean where George and Essie Whidden had a fish house. Edna Earl would stay and play with the Whiddens' daughter, Betty, while Sherrod finished his ice route. He picked her up at the end of the day. "I learned to drive on my daddy's truck. He'd take his 100-pound ice bar, fold it over and put it behind my back so I could reach the accelerator—that's how I learned to drive.

"Two of my playmates were Martha and Jane Weeks. Jane, I remember, always won all the marbles in our games. My biggest thrill was to go to the Seminole Pharmacy, get a cherry smash, go to the show (Desguin's New Movie Theater) and buy a nickel bag of popcorn. Children may have a lot more material things now, a lot more excitement, but it seems to me we had a lot more fun growing up."

Christmas time was always a happy, busy time in the Smith household and this particular day, just before the holidays, Sherrod was rushing to get through his work at the ice house so he could take his wife, Ethel, shopping for last minute gifts. If he hadn't been pressed for time, he never would have made such a careless mistake. "Always turn the machine off when the scorer jaws turn" was the unwritten law of the ice house, but Sherrod, anxious to finish for the day, broke the safety rule. When the mechanism became stuck late in the afternoon and with the machine still running, he tried to loosen the scorer with tongs; the result was the loss of three fingers and part of his hand.

There was no hospital here in those days and Sheriff Quednau drove the injured man to Venice. Momma said she had never been driven so fast in her life. She didn't open her mouth the whole trip!

Sherrod recovered and continued his ice routes, hefting the big blocks of ice with his good hand. "He was a strong man. He used to whack me playfully with his hand in the mornings to wake me up for school. 'Come on honey, time to get up' and it felt like he still had all his fingers!" However, his disability made Sherrod decide to retire when Edna Earl graduated from high school. He didn't make it. In 1947 at the age of fifty-six, he died of a heart attack. Edna Earl graduated the next year, sorely missing the presence of her beloved father.

Sherrod's death left its mark on his widow and daughter, but they carried on. Ethel continued to drive the school bus on the Solana/Burnt Store route and Edna Earl went to work for the Intercounty Telephone Company. She would walk to work past the Princess Hotel porch with its "rocking chair brigade." One of the rockers was a young man with a devil-may-care grin and, eventually, a mutual friend introduced him to Edna Earl. Clayton Poppell worked for the Hercules Powder Company and was in town just temporarily.

Soon the two young people were meeting accidentally on purpose at the Orange Grille and Seminole Pharmacy. On her first formal date with Clayton, Edna Earl stood him up—she had an emergency appendectomy instead. When Dr. Maxwell discharged her from the medical center, the two made up for lost time and soon were seen all over town together.

Edna Earl remembers what a tease he was. "We used to have these portable roller-skating rinks that would come in with a tent and stay for weeks. On our first skating date we went to Arcadia with Jane and

Martha Weeks, Gene Watson and Areta Yeager. Clayton claimed he didn't know how to skate but was game to give it a try. He was all rubbery legs on the floor and the others were exhausted from dragging this inanimate object around the rink. When we finally stopped to rest and get our breath, Clayton took off on his own, executing elaborate figure eights, zooming around with the greatest of ease. He was an excellent skater and had enjoyed to the hilt "putting on" his new friends.

The teasing antics of Clayton grew more serious and romance bloomed; there was a wedding in April 1952. The young couple moved into a house next door to Edna Earl's mother. Clayton had left Hercules Powder to go to work for Slim Keys at his garage across from the courthouse on Taylor Street. Slim confided to his wife, "Mabel, I don't think I can ever make a mechanic out of that boy." That boy went on to become one of the finest mechanics around and made a profitable career in that field.

When a lengthy bout of illness laid Edna Earl low, the natural thing was for the young couple to move in next door with her mother. Ethel was there to take care of her lone "chick" and Clayton and Ethel got along just fine.

Edna Earl's health eventually improved and she returned to work at the telephone company where two of her closest friends, Jane Weeks and Audrey Taylor, were also employed. When the telephone company moved the Punta Gorda "girls" to Fort Myers, Edna Earl stayed put, happily pregnant with the couple's first (and only) child.

Little Sherra Lee (for Grandpa Sherrod) was born in 1954 and Edna Earl settled down to being a housewife and mother. The Poppells also joined in the social life of young marrieds in Punta Gorda. There were movies, visits to the Seminole Pharmacy, occasional dances, barbecues at each other's homes on Saturday nights, with cards afterwards. There were picnics across the river in the woods and fields that are now Port Charlotte; they went on hunting and fishing expeditions and camped out in Frizzell's cow pastures. Life was good.

Slim Keys had by now reversed his opinion of Clayton's mechanical ability and the young man was working full time at Keys' Garage. The relationship was a friendly one in spite of Slim's earlier appraisal of his young apprentice. Clayton worked for him until Slim's death and the subsequent sale of the garage to Sankey Webb. He worked for Sankey until the automobile dealership moved across the river.

Clayton decided to branch out on his own and opened a garage on Carmalita Street between the railroad tracks and U.S. 41. It was a good location. The garage prospered and soon Clayton had Florida Power and Light as one of his customers.

Edna Earl was a busy lady, too, holding down so many part-time jobs that "they were really like a full-time one." She worked part time at the Sallie Jones Elementary School cafeteria, at Charlotte Senior High and the Peace River School. She substituted for Ada on the courthouse switchboard, worked occasionally for Tosie Hindman in the elections office and at the polls, and still found time to work at the Blossom Shop Florists.

This energetic lady also taught Sunday School along with Doreen Cook at the First United Methodist Church for nineteen years "until we began to run out of children."

Children have always been a source of enjoyment to Edna Earl and Clayton. Although Sherra Lee was an only child, she had lots of playmates and the old house on Goldstein was always full of youngsters. Edna Earl reminisces: "Clayton would come home from work dead tired; the neighborhood kids would want a ride in his truck. Clayton would put his shoes back on and off he'd go. He'd never say no."

Clayton sold his garage on Carmalita and opened another, Clayton Two, north of Murdock. In his sixties he still put in a full-day's work, but didn't lose his sense of humor or love of teasing. Sherra Lee lived near her parents and worked for her daddy. Edna Earl worked for more than twelve years at the Blossom Shop "whenever they needed me." She inherited the Smiling Iceman's infectious grin, which broke out repeatedly as she recalled these old Punta Gorda days.

Thriving Black Community

If Benjamin Joshua Baker could be called the pioneer of education in the black community, George Brown was the black pioneer in the business world of this area. He came to Punta Gorda in 1890 with Captain Dewey, owner of a company that brought phosphate by barge down the Peace River.

After his arrival, George branched out on his own, establishing the Cleveland Steam Marine Ways in Cleveland, just upriver from Punta Gorda. He was an eminently successful business man and probably the first "equal opportunity" employer in the vicinity, employing blacks and white alike.

He built an elongated bungalow in Cleveland as a home for his family. Although he owned property on Taylor Street in Punta Gorda, he decided against building a spacious home there, thinking he might be considered "uppity" by the townsfolk. He later sold this piece of land when Punta Gorda was designated the county seat in 1922. The original courthouse was built on property that had been owned by George Brown.

This industrious and popular man operated the Cleveland Steam Marine Ways from the late 1800s to 1930; the facilities of his shipyard could accommodate the largest boats in the Charlotte Harbor vicinity.

One Punta Gordan who had fond recollections of George Brown was Charlie Hurst. Charlie came here in 1925 when he was seven years old. His father, an electrician in New Jersey, had been lured to Punta Gorda by the plentiful jobs offered during Florida's land boom.

Charlie remembers getting off the train at the station, then located across from the big hotel; and walking with his family across the dusty street, past the stately Hotel Punta Gorda and Mobley's Drugstore to Olympia Avenue where his father had rented an apartment. Later, Hurst moved his family to a big, rambling two-story house on the river in the town of Cleveland.

Charlie, his two brothers and three sisters, would ride the school bus along bumpy Marion Avenue to the Taylor Street School. Charlie and his friends spent a lot of time swimming and playing basketball. They also went crabbing and sold the bait crabs to the fishing guides in the area.

Their favorite pastime was working for Mr. George Brown in his shipyard. The boys used burlap bags to scrape the barnacles off the runboats, cleaned up the ever-present debris in the yard and generally made themselves useful. "We worked a little, messed around a little— it gave us something to do and kept us out of trouble."

Wealthy tourists owned large yachts, some requiring a full crew. These boats were hauled up the rails of the shipyard for repairs and for summer storage under tin-roofed sheds. Ship building went on in the yard, too. As Charlie put it, "In those days they built boats 'out of their minds' and no elaborate engineering drawings were needed."

Some of U. S. Cleveland's relatives worked for Brown—Dell was a machinist, Clarence a carpenter and boat builder, Will was also a boat builder and carpenter and Shelby was the man who did the painting and varnishing.

Brown was a man of considerable means, owned the home in Cleveland and his property encompassed what is now the Palms and Pines Trailer Park. He was a friend to all, regardless of color or creed and helped many a family through the hard times of the Depression.

Another thoughtful act endeared him to all the youngsters around. On Saturday nights he would drive the neighborhood children in his big car to Punta Gorda to the movies, delivering them home afterwards. "It wasn't every Saturday night, but at least twice a month. He was a fine man," says Charlie.

* * *

Matthew "Matt" Weeks was born in 1892 to Nicholas and Frances Weeks of Bogue Sound, North Carolina, just south of Harkers Island. The Weeks were a hard-working farm family devoted to the land. Of the large family, Matt was the only one who did not inherit his parents' attachment to the soil. The sea was his love. Work outweighed an education in the Weeks' household and Matt left school after the second grade to work in the fields.

The lure of the sea and faraway places led him to a job on an oil freighter that sailed between Cape Hatteras and Pensacola. His mechanical aptitude and his experience on the tanker enabled Matt to obtain a diesel engineering license and become a full-fledged diesel engineer.

The oil freighter often put into our waters and that is how Matt met his wife-to-be, Mamie Riggs, of Charlotte Harbor. The two were married in June of 1920 and his seafaring days were over.

Matt started Weeks Machine Shop and Boat Works on Long Dock. The young couple moved into a house on Harvey Street, which soon filled with children; William Matthew, Ralph Eugene (died at twenty-one months), Jane, Martha and Wayne. All five were born at home and delivered by Dr. B. B. Blount, assisted by Mrs. Costen, a local nurse.

After the disastrous fire at Long Dock, the city moved the fish houses and related businesses to the Maud Street dock. Wayne remembers, "Dad's shop was where the tennis courts are at Fishermen's Village. The building hung out over the water so that a boom could lift the engines, or even the boats, for overhauling. There was also a boat storage area."

William, known as Billy Matt, is deceased but Jane, Martha and Wayne Weeks reminisced about growing up on Harvey Street. Swimming in the big hotel's outdoor pool was the focal point of every summer. "For ten cents you could swim all day. A teacher, Mrs. Kelly Day, taught us all to swim."

"For spending money we would pull a red wagon full of cow chips garnered from Hendrickson's cows staked in a vacant lot next door. The manure grew beautiful roses and sold for twenty-five cents a wagon load."

Guavas were plentiful in Punta Gorda then and the children alternated loads of fertilizer with sacks of fruit, being careful not to mix the two! Spending money went to the Seminole Pharmacy for ice cream sodas or to McClelland's candy store. "We used to buy marbles at the dime store and Sunday, after church, we'd spend the whole afternoon playing marbles. Jane always used to win them all.

"Saturday nights were special. Dad would give us a quarter apiece before we went downtown. The movie cost nine cents; we saw a serial, a comedy and then the main feature. Mobley's (Seminole Pharmacy) had nickel ice cream cones (two great big dips), popcorn was a nickel and we had change for penny candy—all that for just a quarter."

Matt's boatworks did well, even during the Depression. Wealthy people still wintered in Punta Gorda, spending time and money on their yachts. As the business became established and successful, Matt entered into community affairs, becoming county commissioner and holding that office for twenty-three years.

Mamie was industrious, too. An expert seamstress, she made wedding gowns for many brides in Punta Gorda at that time. She loved to sew, was an avid Baptist Church worker, a great cook and homemaker.

Meanwhile the youngsters were growing up. Martha left school at thirteen to get her beauty license and at age fifteen had her own shop, Milady's Beauty Salon, in the Princess Hotel. Very shortly she married Earis Dunn of Arcadia and they had a daughter, Cynthia. In later years she was married to Judson McCormack, but still continued her work. Martha stated, "I think I'm one of the oldest working beauticians in Charlotte County and I do love my work!"

Jane went with the telephone company after graduation, the switchboard being on the second floor of the old building on the southeast corner of Marion and Taylor. Eventually she, too, got married—to Gene Watson—and left work when their daughter, Sandra Jean, was born.

At the age of fourteen, Wayne was the bellhop at the Princess Hotel and later chauffeured Miss Scull, the owner, around town in her big black Cadillac. During the Korean conflict, he was with the Military Air Transport Service based in Manchester, New Hampshire, where he met his wife, Alice. They have two children, Michelle and Roger, and live in Manchester where Wayne is the owner of a plate glass shop, with another in Salem. His sisters still live in Punta Gorda—Martha in the old homestead and Jane next door. The little red wagon has long since turned to rust but the memories still linger on.

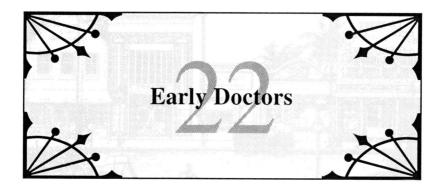

Early Doctors

We've talked about Trabue's early years as a fishing village and cattle town; the arrival of the railroad (and subsequent beginning of the fishing industry here); the building of the big hotel; the renaming of the town to Punta Gorda and the change from a small settlement to a bustling village. We've discussed the first church-school, Miss Norma Pepper's private school and the later public schools and teachers, the first merchants and shopkeepers and small businesses. The next significant new arrivals in town were the professional men: doctors, dentists, lawyers and bankers. Here are some capsule sketches of our early doctors:

Dr. James G. Stephens tightened the reins as the oxcart lumbered down a slippery stretch of the Smoky Mountains. He, his wife, Effie and their two children were making the hazardous trek from Indiana to pioneer a homestead in Florida. It was a long two-and-a-half month journey over the Tennessee hills and Jacksonville looked mighty good to the little family when they stopped there to load their belongings onto the train bound for Arcadia.

Effie and the youngsters boarded in Arcadia while the doctor looked for a suitable piece of land. He had been offered a position as company doctor for a sawmill outfit in the panhandle (Blountstown), but decided the location was too isolated for his family. His children needed playmates, so Dr. Stephens finally settled in Sparkman, an agricultural community about twenty miles due east of Punta Gorda.

James Stephens "doctored" just about everybody in town and delivered all but one of his grandchildren. The exception was Ruth Stephens Allen who was born at the height of the 1926 hurricane. Dr.

Stephens was away at the time and Ruth made her entrance into this world with the help of her grandmother and father. Effie later told her granddaughter that, during Ruth's birth, the floodwaters around the farmhouse were so high that it was continually being lifted off the foundations and then plunked down again!

* * *

Chance meetings often affect the course of one's life. Such was the case when David Norman McQueen, born and raised more than 100 years ago in North Carolina, met H. R. Dreggors. David had worked hard in his brother Neal's sawmill to earn enough money to enroll in the University of Georgia Medical School. While in Augusta, he happened to meet Dreggors. After graduation David finished his internship in New Orleans; then in 1901 he made a trip to Punta Gorda to visit his friend, Dreggors, who with H. W. Smith, had just opened the Punta Gorda Fish Company.

Along with his love of medicine, the young doctor enjoyed outdoor living to the hilt. Punta Gorda with its extensive hunting and fishing seemed the perfect place to hang out his shingle—he stayed. Still a bachelor, David took his meals at the McLane boarding house on Retta Esplanade and another chance encounter changed his life again.

Nathaniel Holderby was a retired lawyer from Carmi, Illinois, and an avid sportsman. Having heard about the excellent turkey hunting in the area, he came here, settling himself in the McLane boarding house. His daughter, Amy, a pretty girl, soon caught the eye of the young doctor. They were married in 1905 and raised a family of five children: Donald, Lucille, Nathaniel, Charles (who died in infancy) and Howard.

Dr. McQueen's life in Punta Gorda was described to us by Nathaniel, better known as "Doc." Not long after learning to walk, little Nathaniel began to accompany his father on house calls, carrying the good doctor's bag that was almost as big as he was! Soon the townsfolk began to jokingly address the tot as "Doc" and the name stuck.

House calls were made by horse and buggy and Doc remembered the faithful steed's name, Old Jim, who was a trotting horse and a good one. Later on, the doctor switched to a Model T Ford.

In the 1920s the McQueen household was often disrupted by emergencies. Dr. McQueen had given up his surgical practice because there was no hospital closer than Arcadia. However, he did perform tonsil-lectomies and repaired broken or mangled limbs. At such times, the dining room table was moved into the parlor and served as the operating table. Later on he "had a little office with operating table, sterilizing equipment, etc. down by the old *Herald* office."

The busy doctor also inspected all personnel of incoming foreign ships for contagious diseases; they were not allowed to dock at Boca Grande until Dr. McQueen had checked everyone on board. He also was state inspector for turpentine stills and lumber yards. Convicts could be "employed" in these establishments for $1 a day and the doctor inspected their sleeping quarters, food and general health.

As if Dr. McQueen wasn't busy enough with his house calls, regular practice, state inspections in the mills and aboard ships, he also began to acquire land. He owned a thirty-acre vegetable farm across from where Banyan Point is now, plus a twenty-five-acre citrus grove up on Shell Creek. The grove would later prove to be a wise investment that "sent all four of us kids to college."

Beside all this, the doctor also owned the Seminole Pharmacy on the corner of Marion Avenue and Taylor Street. The pharmacy was the first combination soda fountain and drug store in the county and he hired Hugh Mobley as his pharmacist. Later on Dr. McQueen sold the pharmacy to Wallace Mobley—and that is why some townsfolks referred to the store as the Seminole Pharmacy while others called it Mobley's Drug Store.

Doc McQueen remembered that many patients paid his father in chickens, mustard greens and sweet potatoes. "Dad received so many chickens, we had to build a fenced-in yard for them out back. One day I was playing in the front of the house when an old man came down the road clutching three or four hens in each hand. 'Boy, where's your chicken yard?' I pointed over my shoulder. 'Back there.' He walked to the backyard and just threw them over the fence."

As busy as the doctor was, he found time for hunting and swimming. He was a good baseball player and a better-than-average tennis player. "When T. C. Crosland built a tennis court by the waterfront near his house, some of the local men formed a club. Dad won the championship for the age bracket of 50 and over."

Ten days before Christmas 1925, Punta Gorda's holiday spirit was dimmed by tragedy. Marion Avenue had been decorated, its shops full of enticing gifts, there were lines at the post office windows and the streets were jammed with traffic. Suddenly in the midst of the holiday rush, two boys were struck down by an automobile in front of the Taylor Street School. As there was no hospital, they were carried to their respective homes and Dr. McQueen was summoned to deal with the double emergency.

The doctor spent the entire afternoon going back and forth across the street tending to the youngsters. "He came home about dark, but said he was too exhausted to eat. I remember him taking a biscuit, crumbling it up in a bowl, pouring milk on it with just a little sugar—that was his supper. I've got to get back over there with the boys," he said and left. There was a theatrical company in town, Jack King's Comedians, and we kids went to the show that night. We got home about 10:30 and were just going to sleep when Momma called Lucille and me and told us to run and get Dr. Blount. Dad was sick. Dad had already taken a syringe from his kit and given himself a shot. When Dr. Blount came, he gave Dad another one. Dad died right there of a heart attack. He was only fifty-five years old."

With his brother, Don, away at college, Doc became head of the McQueen household at age fourteen. While finishing school in Punta Gorda, Doc worked at a grocery store, delivered milk in summer for Brown's Dairy and later substituted as school bus driver for the Prairie Creek-Washington Loop run. He had inherited his late father's energy and predilection to hard work.

After graduating from North Carolina State with a degree in agricultural economics, he became agricultural advisor for Charlotte County. One fateful day, Doc's sister, Lucille, introduced her brother to a pretty fellow teacher, Margaret Brabson, and Doc was a bachelor no more.

Doc and Margaret McQueen had two sons, Robert and John David. Robert is better known in the community as "Bucky" McQueen. Doc used to sing his firstborn to sleep with a popular song of the day "My Little Buckeroo," and the name stuck, just as Doc's nickname stayed with him all his life. Doc held the position of county agricultural agent for thirty-four years. After retiring, he and Margaret lived in a home full of family memorabilia and with a spacious yard so that Doc could still be close to the soil.

* * *

Dr. B. B. Blount was a revered and respected member of his profession, but he was also known around town for his eccentricities. The following anecdotes were told to me by Rupert Carpenter Guthrie, a Charlotte Harbor native.

After you cross over the bridge and sparkling water from Punta Gorda to Charlotte Harbor, a number of shops appear on your right: an automobile dealership, a motorcycle shop and a mower repair service. If you turn into a small street behind these establishments, you are in another time and place.

Here lies a quiet country graveyard with a few shade trees, many headstones, some imposing, some almost hidden in the grass. The quiet is in sharp contrast to hustling, bustling U.S. 41, a scant block away. One family plot contains the graves of the Guthrie family. A stone, nestled in the grass, states FATHER — WILLIAM B. GUTHRIE—1874–1926. Beside it is one for MOTHER—LILLIE JANE, WIFE OF WILLIAM—1871–1926. These are the paternal grandparents of Rupert Carpenter Guthrie—a longtime resident of Punta Gorda.

His grandfather, William Guthrie, came to Charlotte Harbor in 1894, and liked it so well that he returned to North Carolina for his bride and brought her here. By 1895 the couple were settled for good in Charlotte Harbor and raised a family. One son, Rupert Franklin, became a commercial fisherman for his older brother Will, who had founded the Punta Gorda Fish Company with Harry Goulding and Bill Monson.

A young lady from Pine Level, Mabel Locklear, had caught the younger brother's eye and in 1921 Rupert Franklin and Mabel were married and went to live on Bay Street in Charlotte Harbor. In 1930 they had a son, Rupert Carpenter, who became known as "Carpenter." These are his stories of the legendary Dr. Blount.

The good doctor had a two-seater Austin in which he made his house calls. He also had a Pekinese dog, Peewee, who perched on the other seat of the car during the trips to patients. When not on house calls with his master, the little dog trotted all around the town. "Everybody looked after him, he was sort of the town pet."

Peewee also had a running tab in Bill's Bar in Punta Gorda. Anytime the dog walked in, Bill Quednau would pour a bottle of beer into a dish and set it on the floor for Peewee. At the end of the month, Dr. Blount would stop at Bill's Bar and settle his dog's bar bill.

"During prohibition the good doctor was called downtown to treat a lady who had fainted on the sidewalk. He came rattling down there in his old Austin, jumped out and proceeded to raise the swooning woman into a sitting position. 'This is an emergency,' hollered Dr. Blount to the assembled crowd, "has anyone got any spirits?' After some hemming and hawing among the bystanders, a man in the crowd reluctantly passed over a flask. Dr. Blount unscrewed the top, took a hearty swig and pronounced, 'That did the trick! The little lady only fainted; she's much better now."

As Dr. Blount became older, he became more and more absent-minded. One unseasonably cold day in the winter, Dr. Blount had started a toasty fire in the fireplace of his waiting room to make his patients more comfortable. In between consultations, he decided to tidy up his office and, carelessly dumped some shotgun shells (he was an avid hunter) into a wastebasket. Soon the container was filled to the brim with scraps of paper and odds and ends. His nurse, entering the office, noted the overflowing basket, took it into the crowded waiting room and dumped the contents into the crackling fire. Suddenly the room was full of shotgun blasts and people dove under tables and behind chairs to escape the frightening onslaught.

Rumor has it that when Peewee died, Dr. Blount ordered a casket and had the little dog buried in Charlotte Harbor Cemetery. Rumor also has it that, during the night after the burial, someone unearthed Peewee and moved him outside the cemetery boundaries. Enigmatic to the end, nobody was able to find the truth of the matter from Dr. Blount.

* * *

One of the first dentists in town was Vernon Jordan whose father, Adrian, in 1901 became owner of the *Punta Gorda Herald*. Vernon and his brother Julian, (also an aspiring dentist) helped defray their college expenses by opening the first picture show in town. The audience sat on kitchen chairs watching the silent movie and, between reels, Grace Dewey, a friend of the boys, sang.

After Vernon opened his practice in town, he married his sweetheart, Esther Oswald, the youngest teacher for miles around. The wedding was in 1919 and the couple lived happily in Punta Gorda until his death. Years later, Esther married Sam McCullough, a longtime family friend. Mrs. McCullough, or "Miss Esther" as she was fondly known around town, once remarked, "I've been so lucky. I had two good marriages and two wonderful husbands!"

Another professional man in the early days of the town was Dr. E. K. Whidden. Byron Rhode, who arrived in town as a young boy in the early 1900s and whose father, George, was one of our first postmasters, remembers Dr. Whidden mainly because of his car. It was one of the first in town and was called a Brush. It was a one-seater machine with no top and no windshield. It was chain-driven, had hard rubber tires and a tiller for steering. "It looked just like a buggy," said Byron.

Well-known Punta Gorda doctors were: Clement, Kline, and Alexander. Drs. Roscoe Maxwell and Robert Shedd arrived a bit later on the scene and will appear in a chapter on the Medical Center.

Saturday Night in Town

While Punta Gorda was growing from a frontier settlement into a small established town, social activities centered around the church. As we've noted, the first school was church-sponsored, as were community get-togethers, barbecues, quilting bees and the like. Young people used the church as a meeting place and many marriages were from a "church courtship." Other popular activities were cane-grinding parties and swimming in the bay was always an excuse for a picnic.

Charlie Hurst, who grew up in the little town of Cleveland and gave us the vivid description of George Brown and his shipyard, remembers the dancing in Cleveland and old Punta Gorda. "On Saturday nights we'd all get together at somebody's house for square dancing—little tykes, parents, grandparents, teenagers—all together. It was great fun!"

Minta Hopper Harper, a retired teacher who came here as a child in 1913 has many memories of the social activities of life in those days. Out on Shell Creek where she grew up, lazy summer days were spent fishing in the creek, swimming off her backyard, playing croquet, having sugar cane threshing parties and overnight camping trips.

Minta's stepfather, Slade Lanier, owned a large rambling house on the creek and the young people of Cleveland and Punta Gorda liked to congregate there. Minta's mother, Rose, had purchased a piano with some of her teaching money and Minta would play while her friends danced or sang the popular tunes of the day.

"Sometimes, after a night of dancing, we'd get in our boat and row upstream. The water was very phosphorus in those days and at night the fish glowed, skimming under the surface; it was like a fairyland."

Saturday night was *the night* in Punta Gorda in the early years of our town. Murry Hall recalls it as if it were yesterday.

Murry was a late Christmas present to the Hall family in Charlotte Harbor. He was born on December 26, 1909, and had ten brothers and sisters. Life was very different in Charlotte Harbor then; there was as yet no bridge linking it to Punta Gorda and anyone needing a doctor had to sail across the bay to fetch him. There were few motor boats around. If there was no wind, medical help might be a long time coming and the midwife was kept busy. People were forced to be self-sufficient and events we take for granted were cherished occasions then.

Saturday was just such an occasion in Murry's young life. Saturday was the day for going to Punta Gorda. As early as nine o'clock in the morning, people—cattle ranchers, fishermen, farmers, housewives and children—would start pouring into town from miles around.

They came by boat, truck, wagon, on horseback and even on foot. Everyone rushed to get a parking place and the benches and boardwalks on the main streets of town were full to overflowing. People had worked hard all week and this was their day to visit, gossip, swap stories, meet old friends, do a little business and shop.

All the stores stayed open until late; Mobley's Drug Store didn't close until almost midnight and the movie house did a brisk business. This was in the roaring twenties and, although Punta Gorda didn't actually roar at midnight, the town was still very much alive!

Murry was fortunate enough to have an older friend, Claude Willis, whose father ran the mail boat from Charlotte Harbor to Punta Gorda and back. Claude was courting a Miss Alma Howland of Punta Gorda and he let Murry and his friends ride over in the mail boat on Saturdays.

The youngsters would go to the movies, then drop in at Mobley's for ice cream. Later, they would stroll down to the dock to await the skipper. Claude eventually married Miss Alma so the trips were not in vain!

Another memory of Saturday nights belonged to Clara Hobson Rickard. Clara, a tiny wisp of a woman with a twinkle in her eye and a pure enjoyment of life in spite of the rough and bumpy road she has traveled remembered the following: In 1896 she was born in Cleveland to John and Sally Hobson, one of eight children. Their father homesteaded eighty acres and in 1898 moved the family to Shell Creek. John Hobson worked hard in his two orange groves and all the children pitched in as soon as they were old enough. Sally, worn out from years of hard work and childbearing, died when Clara was six. Her older sisters divided the household chores between them while still attending school. One of the older boys or their father would drive to the little country school by horse and buggy.

John Hobson and his family lived off the land. He had planted two orange groves, one right beside the big white house and another a short distance away. The Hobsons raised chickens and grew their own vegetables. The boys made crates for the fruit and packed the oranges out in the groves. Their father carried them to town where the fruit was shipped to distant places, far from Punta Gorda.

Clara helped pack the eggs every week, twelve to fifteen dozen, and her father took them to town on Saturday to sell to merchants always ready to receive fresh eggs and other produce.

"Every Friday night after supper we would gather around the kitchen table and shell cow peas—about twenty quarts of them. Daddy would take them to town Saturday morning after an early breakfast, along with the eggs and other vegetables and, oh yes, watermelons! We would sell watermelons for twenty-five cents and be tickled to death to get it."

Clara remembers the roads her daddy traveled to town were just sandy ruts. There were no paved roads then even in town. "He would spend the whole day doing our shopping and wouldn't get home 'til nearly dark."

* * *

Fritz Quednau bought a tract of land from Colonel Isaac Trabue in 1892 and his grandson, Albert, treasured a piece of paper signed by Fritz and the colonel attesting to that fact. The original house on this property was a two-story structure of eleven rooms. In later years Albert and Argo Whidden, a local carpenter, remodeled it into a one-story house. Albert and his wife lived there at the time this book was written in 1987.

As a boy, Albert grew up on Virginia Avenue. The railroad that ran down to the fish docks was right in back of his house. He and the Cleveland boys spent many happy hours playing on the railroad grade, digging caves and waging imaginary battles with cow chips for ammunition. The area around Punta Gorda was truly "a happy hunting ground" and Albert grew up tracking wild turkey, quail, wild hogs, squirrels and occasionally deer. A. C. Frizzell's pasture land was an excellent freshwater fishing spot and, although his land was fenced for cattle, he looked the other way when the boys went hunting there.

Life wasn't all play for Albert, however, and his recollections of Saturday nights in town were of hard work. In the afternoons after school, he delivered groceries and stocked shelves in Vasco and Lois Peeples' IGA store. Albert played football on Friday nights and, because of this, Vasco and Lois let him come in a bit later on Saturday mornings. Even so, Albert dreaded Saturdays. "The town was always full of people and they'd wait until the last possible minute to do their grocery shopping." The young boy wouldn't start cleaning up the vegetable bins until 10:00 P.M. or later. Sometimes he wouldn't get home before two in the morning.

Saturday nights were a busy time for Larue Earnest, the barber. He was born in Punta Gorda and met his wife-to-be, Lillian Sprott, in Boca Grande where her father owned the Boca Grande ferry. The newlyweds moved to Sebring where Larue worked as a barber. However, after the birth of a son, Larue, he had decided to come back to his hometown. When there was an opening in the Princess Hotel's barber shop in 1936, Larue moved back home. A couple of years later Larue opened his own barbershop on Marion Avenue.

Larue's widow recalled that the farmers would drive in at dawn on Saturday, some in wagons and trucks, some in cars. They staked out their special parking place and set out on foot to visit with friends, do some business, shop, eat, go to the movies and get a haircut. Grocery shopping and the barber were last on the list after the movie house "let out" and Larue was often still cutting hair at 11:00 P.M. When you look at Punta Gorda on Saturday nights now, everything seems to close up quite early in the evening. It is hard to visualize the hustle and bustle that used to go on downtown fifty years ago!

Traveling tent shows were an important part of the life of the town and provided much needed entertainment. The pupils of the Taylor Street School were fortunately attending a traveling circus show the day the school burned to the ground. There were many of these tent shows and children were often excused from school to enjoy them. Mrs. Mary Maxwell of Maxwell's Pharmacy recalls one such tent show in Gilchrist Park, in front of her home, featuring elephants. The lumbering beasts left noticeably potent reminders of their visit.

Mary Agnes Crosland Fambrough recalls that periodically Jack King's Comedians would come to Punta Gorda and erect a big tent on a vacant lot on Marion Avenue. Although the show seldom changed and the jokes were always the same, the "Comedians" played to standing room only. It was Florida's answer to vaudeville.

Maude Mauck of Charlotte Harbor has an amusing comment on the entertainment of the times. In 1921 when the first bridge was built between Charlotte Harbor and Punta Gorda, the approaches to it were not paved. A man with a team of mules used to station himself there to pull the cars out of the sand when they got stuck. People used to come to watch this free side show!

There was a more orthodox form of entertainment that Maude remembers: the tent shows that came three or four times a year; the Williams Stock Company was one. These stock companies staged plays with musical entertainment in between the acts. There was an occasional black minstrel show, which was always popular, and traveling circuses came to town, too. Maude laughingly recalls elephants sashaying down Marion Avenue.

Joe Addison, who raced his pony across the sand flats (later to become Punta Gorda Isles) has fond memories of the minstrel show's arrival in town. When Silas Green from New Orleans and the Rabbit Foot Minstrels arrived they would strut up and down the streets playing their Dixieland Jazz to lure people to their tent shows. Marching right along with them would be little Joe Addison who played hooky from school to join in the excitement. He was an avid drummer, using cast-off chair rungs as sticks and a tin pan for a drum.

Ed Smith, a trombone player, had organized a local "marching band' in which J. T. Rose (later to become a judge) played the saxophone and

Joe's cousin, Norman Cochran, the snare drum. "I was a little runt and they wouldn't let me play—besides, I didn't have a real drum. One night Norman got sick. They needed a drummer and let me play his snare." That was one of the highlights of Joe's childhood. He noted wistfully that he wished his father, who loved jazz and the blues, could have lived to hear Joe beat the drum that night.

Joe graduated form high school in 1926 and, looking for ways to make money for college, he landed a job at the post office as substitute clerk at sixty cents an hour. Working at this job for a year and a half, he saved enough money to buy a real drum and enter the University of Florida.

While at college, Joe defrayed some of his expenses by playing with the Gator Collegians, a twelve-piece band that played at dances. He also "hopped" tables at Miss Cobb's boarding house "in order to get something to eat." Joe had to guarantee at least five boys daily at his table in order to keep his job; Leo Wotitzky was one of his "eaters." "The food was terrible, but Leo stuck by me through thick and thin and I've never forgotten that."

When the stock market crash came and banks folded, Joe had to quit college and come home. The young man took work where he could find it, including pumping gas at the Gulf Station in Punta Gorda. He married a "little girl from Alabama," Moselle Weathers, and settled into married life. Shortly after the wedding Joe returned to the post office as money order clerk, then finance clerk. When Postmaster Dewey died in office in 1950, Joe became acting postmaster and served in this position until the appointment of Hugh MacGibbon as postmaster. Joe then became rural carrier for Route 1 and continued in this job until his retirement in 1975.

During these years Joe moonlighted as a drummer with various local bands, most of the time playing with Fred Stollsteimer's group. Eventually he put together his own "Joe Addison's Combo" and performed at the Port Charlotte Yacht Club and the Punta Gorda Country Club.

Moselle and Joe had thirty-nine happy years together until her death in 1972. Later he remarried and lived with Marian and two "best friends" (a shepherd and a bird dog) on Virginia Avenue 190 feet from his boyhood home. Joe remembered well those long-ago minstrel shows with the bands strutting down Marion Avenue and the excitement in the air.

* * *

Another form of entertainment a little on the unusual side, such as watching the man with the mule team pull sand-bogged automobiles from the entrance to the "new" bridge, was "The Liars' Corner." Albert Quednau remembers it well. When I asked Albert what he misses most about the old days in Punta Gorda, he replied, "the small town atmosphere of friendliness and sociability. Everybody knew everybody." There was only one traffic light in town and that was at the corner of Marion Avenue and U.S. 41. This corner became known as "Liars' Corner," because almost every evening Sheriff Fred Quednau (Albert's uncle), Chief of Police Sim Holt, Fire Chief Henry Koon and other old-timers used to gather there and swap tall tales. Today, at U.S. 41 and Marion Avenue, people don't stop to sit and talk, they are too busy rushing by in their cars to make the light.

There was a time long ago in Punta Gorda when the arrival of the evening mail train was a social event enjoyed by all the townsfolk. It was an established custom of the day to go to Maxwell's Pharmacy in the new arcade to have a coke, cherry smash or a dish of ice cream while waiting for the mail to be sorted. It wasn't until January of 1952 that there was city delivery and the first rural delivery wasn't until October of that same year.

Maxwell's Pharmacy, as mentioned earlier, was owned by Roscoe "Mack" Maxwell, a handsome and popular man who played "host" at this evening gathering. A lady who has lived in Punta Gorda since 1952 arrived just before the inception of mail delivery and enjoyed the evening mail custom. "We were city folk and used to having mail delivered to our door. Now we'd join the others at Maxwell's Drug Store, have a soda or ice cream and wait for the mail. It was truly a social occasion and we, along with the rest of the town, looked forward to it."

This same woman remembers there was a group of adventurous young couples ("out of town" on McKenzie Street near the high school) who owned horses and had a great time riding around the countryside. The men fixed up a stable of sorts near the school bus garage and every weekend there was an outing. "We went on riding parties; one person followed with a jeep loaded with food and beverages. He would drive to a designated pasture and we'd have a barbecue. The jeep driver would swap his vehicle for a horse and someone else would drive the jeep back to town. We called ourselves the Aching Tail Riding Club. Anyone who could beg, borrow or steal a horse was welcome at these parties. One time we made the mistake of offering our backyard as the meeting place. Fifteen or twenty horsemen showed up that day and we had to put in a new backyard!"

She also recalled that when a child had a birthday, the party was usually held on the Hotel Charlotte Harbor's beachfront at the umbrella tables or elsewhere on the hotel grounds. Grown-up parties were held at the hotel as well and were dressy, "posh" affairs in the ballroom after delicious dinners concocted by the talented but temperamental chef. She well remembers the night the "grand old lady" burned. "The whole town was aglow, everything fiery red; no one slept that night."

In the 1930s when "Little Doc" and Faye Whitehurst were growing up, politics was as much an entertainment form as anything else. Their father, "Doc" Whitehurst, was an engineer on one of T. C. Crosland's runboats and Faye remembers that he loved politics and Leo Wotitzky was one of his best friends. When Leo was running for state representative, Doc would often travel as far as Englewood or Gasparilla Island, way out in the boondocks, to hear Leo speak. He wouldn't get back home until after his children had gone to bed.

One morning after a political rally away from home, Faye cornered her father at breakfast. "Daddy, how did the rally go?" "Just fine," was the reply. "How many people were there?" "About five or six." "*About five or six?*" "Yup, but Leo gave them *the whole thing!*"

Nowadays, at election time, there are the usual "coffees," letters to the editors, pamphlets stuck in our door or on the car windshield and the inevitable political signs planted all over town. "Little Doc" Whitehurst remembers that back in the old days there was much more whooping and hollering in the city streets. Election rallies were big in those days.

When running for office, politicians would hold rallies every other week. Each candidate would be given so much time to speak. They'd hold a rally in the middle of Marion Avenue by the Seminole Pharmacy, or on the football field, on a street corner in Charlotte Harbor or in a field in Englewood.

E. H. "Scotty" Scott, clerk of the court, was a well-known and popular emcee at these things. He would keep the crowd in fine fettle with his humorous introductions, roasting all the candidates with his dry wit. Scotty described one popular, though long-winded orator, as being "like the Mississippi River, big at the mouth and always flowing." Candidates took these ribbings good naturedly as a part of the game of politics.

After elections were over, the town celebrated by building political "graveyards" for the losers in any vacant lot they could find. People would come into town the day after an election to place appropriate wooden "headstones" for the defeated candidate on mounds of newly dug earth. There might be twenty-five or more "Here lies. . . . Most inscriptions were done in a friendly, jovial vein, some were hopefully plotted and cunningly contrived weeks in advance. A few were on the vitriolic side and provoked hard feelings and long-running feuds. Whatever the outcome, heavy debates, fervent interest and neighborhood awareness were the order of the day. Voter turnout was much heavier in those days.

When the portable roller-skating rinks finally came to the area, they did a brisk business. For one Punta Gorda couple, Edna Earl and Clayton Poppell, roller skating parties played a big part in their courtship. Edna Earl still talks of one of their first dates when they went to Arcadia to roller skate.

Nancy Lawhorne (Raulerson) of Lawhorne's Food Palace remembers her early dates with husband-to-be, Jerry. From the tenth grade on, Jerry and Nancy had been a twosome, going to the Breezeway Drive-In, the Seminole Pharmacy, Nagy's Drugstore and skating at Newall's Portable Skating Rink.

Ever since the motion picture was invented, it had been a prime source of entertainment. The first movie house, a brainstorm of Vernon Jordan and his brother, Julian, was in a rented storefront on Marion Avenue. They were the sons of Adrian Jordan, owner of the *Punta Gorda Herald*. They used the money from this enterprise to help defray their expenses at college. The boys kept expenses to a minimum, seating the audience on kitchen chairs, but they did invest in a piano, which a friend played during the program. Another friend, Grace Dewey, sang at intermission and their sister took the tickets. They did well, sold the business to Harry Goldstein and went off to dentistry college.

After Vernon became Dr. Jordan and returned home he became smitten with a pretty newcomer, a sixteen-year old teacher, Miss Esther Oswald. Esther lived in Solana, just outside Punta Gorda, but taught in Charlotte Harbor. This was in 1914 and there was no bridge across the bay. Esther took the mail boat every Monday morning; she boarded in Charlotte Harbor during the school week, returning on Friday afternoon. She always had a date on Friday evening, often with young Dr. Jordan, and they usually went to the picture show. Esther's favorite was the serial, "The Perils of Pauline."

Belle McBean (Quednau), Cap'n Fred's wife and Tosie Hindman's mother, can think of a great many happy times in her childhood but a special treat was going to Harry Goldstein's picture show. It was fun to watch the "silents" and there was musical entertainment in between reels. It only cost a dime! After the show, there was Mobley's Seminole Pharmacy for a great big soda (a dime) or a nickel ice cream cone.

In 1936, there was a ten-year-old boy in Oneida, New York, who wasn't a bit happy about selling his pony and moving to a little town in Florida with a funny name. His father had decided to leave his job with Oneida Silver to operate a movie theater in Punta Gorda on the advice of his brother who already owned a chain of theaters in the state.

So it was with many misgivings on September 9, 1936 that L. Victor "Vic" Desguin, age ten, came with his family to live in a big white house on the corner of Olympia Avenue and Sullivan Street. The movie house was called the New Movie Theater and was located where the parking lot for Ace Hardware is now.

Soon the New Theater was running full tilt as a family operation. Vic's parents sold the tickets and supervised the shows. Vic and his brother ran the popcorn concession. The boys' Uncle Fred had given them a popcorn machine as a joint birthday present and also the popcorn concessions in his theaters in Sebring, Avon Park, Wauchula, Fort Meade and Mulberry. At the grand old age of ten, Vic and his brother had their own business called the Des Mul Confection Company!

"The only thing we sold in the theater was popcorn, so we'd let people go down the street to the Seminole Pharmacy to buy their candy and cold drinks to have during the show." Of course, they were supposed to buy popcorn. Are you beginning to get the picture of what a family town Punta Gorda was back then?

Mosquitoes were very prevalent in Punta Gorda before the introduction of mosquito control and aerial spraying. "When people walked down the street they would carry a switch of Australian pine (it has long sharp needles) or a towel and they just kept popping them to keep the mosquitoes on the wing. We had screens on the movie house doors, which helped a little, and the biggest Flit spray gun I've ever seen. You could pump under pressure and it would spray forever. We would go down the aisles with that thing and people would stick out their legs and feet so you could spray them, too!"

The Desguins had a huge blower to start the air circulating before the audience arrived. One Sunday afternoon Vic turned on the blower and, after it made one complete turn, he heard an ear-piercing shriek and a cat came flying out of it into the empty theater. The terrified animal had been catnapping in the big fan; it took almost twenty minutes to corner the hysterical feline and usher it out the door.

The New Theater changed movies every two days with a single on Saturday and a matinee on Sunday afternoon. Saturday was *the day* in Punta Gorda and Vic remembers how the people used to crowd into town. He even remembers seeing mule-drawn carts! Family schedules revolved around show time. On Saturdays the doors opened shortly after five with three continuous shows, letting out around eleven. Parents would drop their kids off at the theater and most of them stayed for all three shows! Families in town for the weekly visit with friends and shopping would wait until a half hour before the show closed to buy their meat and perishables, making the grocery stores late in closing. Then people would load up their cars with groceries and stop by the show to pick up the kids and take them home. "Sometimes we had kids whose parents just plain forgot them and they would spend the night at our house." Literally, Punta Gorda was one big family while Vic Desguin was growing up here.

* * *

Punta Gorda, like all southern towns in the 1930s, was not integrated. The Desguins had lived in Oneida, New York, with only one black family in town. Now they were faced with the problem of a segregated black community eager to see their movie shows. Vic's father solved the dilemma by making use of an old tin building out on Charlotte Avenue in the "quarters." He built some wooden benches, bleacher-type seats, bought a 35mm projector and started to show movies one night a week.

"Dad would drive out there on a Wednesday evening, taking the cartoon feature with him, and start selling tickets." Meanwhile young Vic would grab the first reel of the feature movie in the New Theater as soon as it came off the projector, rewind it, stow it in a metal case on his bike and pedal to the Charlotte Avenue building. "Dad would begin the cartoon with twenty minutes of the feature handy and I would pedal back for reel three while my brother was delivering reel two on his bike. We would alternate like that, shuttling back and forth, until the feature was over. Then we'd pedal home, plop into bed with school ahead of us in the morning. For years and years I can remember little black kids pointing me out, 'there goes the picture-show boy.'"

On Saturdays, the "picture-show boy" played as hard as he worked, tennis with his pals on the old hotel grounds, fishing in Alligator Creek and had the most fun of all in a twelve-foot skiff. "There'd be seven or eight of us boys, crammed into that boat, some rowing, some hanging onto the sides in inner tubes. We'd take our lunch and row from 'Buzzards Roost' in Gilchrist Park to the other side of the bay where Bay Marina is now. We'd stay there all day, swimming, eating a picnic lunch, floating lazily in our inner tubes, just fooling around till it was time to row back home for our supper." This, then, was the busy but happy childhood of "the picture-show boy."

When the war came, Vic enlisted in the Navy; after his discharge he enrolled at the University of Florida. In 1951 he married Peggy Rigell (Rigell Lumber and Supply), bought a home on Melbourne Street right by the river and raised a family of six children, five boys and a girl. He went back into the theater business with his father and also managed the Charlotte County Chamber of Commerce in Punta Gorda from 1955 to 1958. Then the Desguins bought a drive-in theater in

Charlotte Harbor. Vic operated that while his father ran the theater in Punta Gorda.

In 1968 the drive-in closed to make room for the Town and Country Shopping Center.

While Vic ran the drive-in he had also been working from 1965 on for Mrs. Areta Yeager in the tax collector's office. When she retired in 1972, Governor Rubin Askew appointed Vic Desguin as tax collector of Charlotte County and he served in that capacity for many years.

Vic is very content in the Peace River area. In fact, he has made this his home for fifty years and raised his large family here. His wife, Peggy died in 1976 when their youngest child, Larry, was only eight. This left Vic a widower with six children. In 1980 he remarried and his wife, Charlotte, has a son, Shane, whom Vic adopted.

Wayne Weeks remembers the Desguins movie house as one of his favorite places. He also remembers that his dad, Matt, (Weeks Machine Shop and Boat Works) always gave his children a quarter apiece before they went to town on Saturday night. Nine cents of that went to the movies and the rest on Mobley's ice cream and Vic's popcorn. Sometimes the children spent more than he anticipated, and, since he enjoyed westerns, he would often pop into the movies with extra change in case the youngsters needed it. "Dad always had a pocketful of change and, when I'd hear the jingle of coins in the back of the theater, it meant that Dad was there. It also meant I'd better behave!"

Mrs. Mary Maxwell of Maxwell's Pharmacy has another memory of the Desguin theater. "Our son, Richard, (now a noted dental surgeon in Atlanta), loved to go to the Desguins' movie house. Mrs. Desguin was a favorite of the town's youngsters. Though she brooked no nonsense such as running in the aisles, she mothered the children like her own. Admission price for those under twelve was nine cents; after twelve the price went up. After his twelfth birthday, Richard approached the ticket window, 'Mrs. Desguin, I'm twelve years old now." The dear lady replied, "Well now, Richard, let's forget it for a few weeks anyway." There again you have the family feeling of old Punta Gorda.

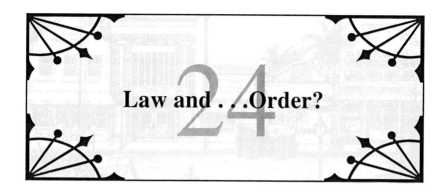

Law and . . .Order?

Law and order came slowly to the little settlement of Trabue/Punta Gorda. Kelly Harvey, the original surveyor of Trabue described the village as "overrun with bums, riffraff, gamblers, toughs and adventurers. There were five murders in the year 1886 alone." The first lock-up was an old boxcar and it was usually filled. In 1904 City Marshal John Bowman was gunned down in his own living room while playing with his children! The Marshall had been for a long time in the pursuit of a gang of thugs, the "Tigermen," but they managed to ambush him instead.

Eventually the gangs were put out of action and the main problem was the wild and raucous cowboys and fishermen letting off steam after a weeks hard work by boozing it up on Saturday night. The ensuing street fights were becoming too numerous and the city fathers saw that some place of restraint was sorely needed. To handle this unruly group, the town built a portable cage with steel bars and placed it on Olympia Avenue across from where the telephone office is now. In this primitive jail, wrongdoers were exposed to the taunts and jeers of the townsfolk. Now, many of these "criminals" were hard-working fishermen and their jobs were dependent on their reporting to the fishing boats by 4:00 A.M. on Monday.

In the 1920s, Ira Atkinson was a man of many hats. He answered fire alarms while on duty as a policeman, was truant officer of schools and recorder of marks and brands (of cattle). During these years the inmates of the portable cage were mostly drunks who refused Ira's advice to go home and sober up. One of these men was a carpenter and fisherman who had helped build the calaboose. The story goes that one

Sunday night, he became very belligerent after consuming a large portion of the town's liquor supply and was thrown in the clink. Once inside he made threats to the world at large, adding that "they" couldn't keep him in there!

He was right. In broad daylight, with his carpentry skills he unscrewed a few boards and exited through the roof. Standing in full view of the passersby he flapped his arms energetically, crowed like a rooster, and jumped off the roof. By dawn's early light he was out on the bay with his fellow fishermen.

As truant officer, Ira Atkinson had a way with kids, probably because he liked them. In 1921 when he was appointed Sheriff Jim Lipscomb's deputy, his relationship with the town youngsters came in handy on more than one occasion. For example, a young friend of his remarked that something peculiar was going on at school and he thought it might be dope. Ira investigated and found that marijuana was being brought in by shrimp boat from Campeche, Mexico.

The federal authorities in Tampa were notified that the boat should be checked when it docked in Punta Gorda. There was a leak somewhere along the line and the smugglers were alerted by ship-to-shore that the feds were awaiting them in Punta Gorda. They turned the boat around and headed into Tampa, but the Punta Gorda sheriff's department and the federal authorities had already anticipated this switch. The ship was seized in Tampa with all the contraband aboard. This was the end, for a long time, of the drug drops in the area.

However, there was a much lighter side to Ira's duties as the policeman of Punta Gorda. One day, during the boom in 1925, there was a free fish fry held in back of the old hotel. Traffic was snarled up for blocks and Ira, as the one policeman, had his hands full.

In the midst of all this chaos, several irate citizens complained to him about a man from Sarasota, drunk, belligerent and generally raising cain. "I'll get to him in a minute," said Ira. "I'm too busy right now." Just then, a heavy hand clapped him on the back and a raucous voice bellowed, "Are you a cop? In Sarasota, if I want a drink, the cops get it for me!" This man, of course, was the drunken menace.

"Yes, I'm a police officer," said Ira, "and I want you to feel right at home. If you'll just follow me, I've got a five-gallon demijohn in a house around the corner and you're welcome to drink as much as you want."

Happy and content, the reeling visitor docilely followed Ira around the corner where he was ushered graciously into the calaboose. Ira slammed the door, barred and padlocked it. This was a successful psychological ploy which had to work as the stranger weighed around 200 pounds to Ira's scant 112!

For the next half century the town began to thrive on its fishing industry, cattle raising and shipment of citrus fruits. The railroad linked us to the northern markets and we had the rising status of being a deep water port. Also, the Hotel Punta Gorda was bringing in affluent people, "big-time spenders" from far and wide. Lured by this prosperity, a new breed of criminal began to seep into town and "The Cage" was no longer feasible.

U. S. Cleveland remembers that the second floor of the new County Courthouse was devoted to the jail. There were two cell blocks, each with four cells, four bunks in each with a corridor connecting them. Cell doors and the corridor door were controlled by levers in the hallway in their own locking cabinets. There were also three or four individual cells opening off the corridor leading to the courthouse. He thought that each of these also had four bunks. Bunks were suspended from sides of the cells and could be folded up out of the way—double-decker style. The courtroom door was heavy steel with barred peep holes. The stairway from the Olympia Avenue entrance led only to the jail where there was a large steel door—also with barred peep hole.

Sheriff Fred Quednau had a long row to hoe. He was a hard-working but understaffed officer; he had no official patrol car and he and his deputies were "plainclothesmen" because there were no uniforms.

Sheriff Quednau went on to become mayor of the town and Travis Parnell in 1957 took over the reins as sheriff. He drove his own car for a while, then bought two patrol cars for which the county eventually reimbursed him. Travis and his deputies finally got uniforms and, with the help of public-spirited citizens, he purchased the harbor's first patrol boat. It was used not only to capture smugglers and other fugitives but also in rescue operations. Sheriff Parnell was a man of few words but much action. He earned the respect of his peers.

Meanwhile, his wife, Maud, took over as matron; a title that encompassed myriad duties. She did all the cooking for the forty-two or more prisoners on a kerosene stove that defies description. It had four burners and a tin box contraption to set on top for an oven. When the "oven" was in use, she was down to two burners for the rest of the meal! Maud also served as jailer when her husband's duties called him away. Often she had to interrupt her baking to fingerprint a new inmate—a little frustrating to say the least, particularly with the smell of burning bread in the oven.

Fortunately, Maud Parnell had a sense of humor that saw her through those pioneer days at the jail. There were unusual problems. One female inmate named Billie refused to wear any clothes in the heat of the summer and sat in her cell in the "altogether." A young trusty, in charge of serving meals, particularly enjoyed serving Billie. When Maud learned about Billie's dishabille she told her, "No clothes, no food!" Billie dressed for dinner after that!

Maud had a surprising number of happy, rather than unpleasant, memories of those early times in the "new" jail. She talked kindly of her "boys" and mentioned that she still heard from many of them at Christmas time. Even those spending time in a cell in our little town seemed to find that family feeling.

When she was delivering newspapers in town, Mattie May McDaniel (Hughes) recalls that she used to wait for the *Tampa Tribune* truck in the wee hours of the morning. The Gulf Station on U.S. 41 was a sheltered spot and, when the papers arrived, she'd sit under its protective roof and roll her papers. Keeping her company would be Sim Holt, the chief of police, who sat there at night "watching over the town, though there wasn't much town to watch then." The two of them would chat about the day's events, personal happenings and so forth while the town slept.

Alto Orr, who came to Punta Gorda in 1938, had a most unusual childhood. His father, Jack, spent fifty-eight years traveling with circuses and at one time owned many acres of Panama City—land deals he made through his circus contacts. Using Panama City as a base, he and a partner imported animals from South America for the circus acts. One day Jack discovered, from the babblings of a drunken captain, that there were false bottoms in the animal cages and that his partner was engaged in rumrunning operations, using the circus as a cover-up. Jack tore out the false bottoms, fired the captain and suffered his partner's revenge.

The revenge was sweet. The partner drained the oil from the engines. Halfway out of the harbor, the boat caught fire from the overheated engines and was demolished. That was the end of Jack Orr's Panama City operation and he headed south to join the American Circus Association.

Alto Orr was born in Alabama and arrived with his family in Punta Gorda in 1938. Physically fit, because of his early training in his father's circus activities, Alto was very involved in school athletics, particularly football and softball. He had a talent for striking out every batter he faced, In one instance, our high school team played an Army team stationed here and Alto pitched a no-hitter against them.

As he modestly explains, "Can you figure out how you could hit a ball off a kid who's been throwing knives in a sideshow since he was nine years old? The knives I was throwing weighed a pound and a quarter!"

Alto went on to join the Naval Air Force at sixteen (he seemed to be the proverbial early bird in everything) and returned home to Punta Gorda when he was nineteen. Having been an ardent fisherman, when he wasn't throwing knives and pitching no-hitters, he went into the fishing guide business. At the peak of the season, he remembers he "sold" three days to the Hotel Charlotte Harbor, two days to the Eagle's Nest and kept two days for personal clients. In the summer he was back on the road with the carnival. Alto figures that, at one time or another, he was connected with every legitimate carnival show on the eastern seaboard.

In later years, Alto ran a service station, owned a hardware store, was postmaster of Charlotte Harbor and operated a profitable real estate business. He married Amanda Kennedy who was a staunch supporter of all his wide and varied interests in life. Alto and his wife lived for many years in a pastoral setting on Shell Creek.

In case you are wondering how Alto Orr wandered into this chapter on law and order, here is one of his favorite stories. "Punta Gorda was a sleepy little town, except in tourist season. How sleepy was it? Alto chuckles, "It was 1945 and I had just come home from the service. I was driving on Marion and started to back up, trying to navigate around two badly parked cars so I could stop at the Village Restaurant (now Waldo's Bistro). We had three police officers in all of Charlotte County at that time: Sheriff Quednau, Chief of Police Sim Holt and Ira Atkinson who was then the deputy city policeman. Mr. Atkinson now appeared beside my car and informed me that it was illegal to back up more than twenty feet within the city limits. "Mr. Atkinson," I said, "I want you to look up and down Marion as far as you can see. There are three automobiles on this entire street. One of these is yours, one belongs to the young man who runs the hardware store and the other is mine. Now I want you to tell me something else. Can you see one chicken, one cow, one dog, cat or human being on this entire street except for the two of us? Now, pray tell me, what or whom am I going to run over?" I don't believe Ira gave Alto a ticket.

We came a long way from the calaboose, from Sheriff Quednau's "plainclothesmen," Travis Parnell's first harbor boat to a debate in town over the use of a helicopter!

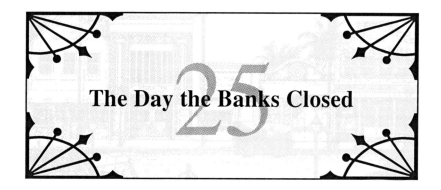

The Day the Banks Closed

The Great Depression came to Punta Gorda as it did to many sleepy insular southern towns with a sharp period of panic and then a rude awakening to the outside world.

One of the people affected by it was a young woman of Charlotte Harbor, Maude Dick. Her family put down roots in the area as far back as 1888. She remembers a tale her father told:

A panther snarled as it stalked the campfire and the lone guard nervously shifted his rifle. Her father, then a young boy stirred rest-lessly in his family's covered wagon and wondered again if they had done the right thing in leaving Louisiana for this faraway place. The year was 1888, the young boy's name was Ralph Dick and he and his family were spending their first night in the newly named town of Punta Gorda. They were encamped on the spot where Perry McAdow was later to plant the famous banyan tree and where the Best Western now stands.

In 1883 another family, the Currys, had arrived from Indiana in a more conventional way. They had taken the train to Cedar Key and transferred to a boat which brought them to the small village of Harbor View just across the bay from Punta Gorda. William Curry and his progeny lived in Harbor View for many years; then, as the family grew, Hiram Curry moved by boat to Punta Gorda.

The Dick and Curry families became acquainted and, in 1892, Rose Curry and Ralph Dick were married. The newlyweds lived here in Punta Gorda until 1898 when they moved to Texas where a daughter, Maude, was born. In 1920 Rose and her daughter came back to Florida and settled in Charlotte Harbor. Maude was now twenty years old and a very progressive young woman for those days. She didn't sit home and wait to get married, but set out into the business world.

In 1922 Maude became bookkeeper for the First National Bank of Punta Gorda and stayed there until transferred to the Fidelity Trust. She was working there when the Depression forced the banks to close— a time she will never forget.

"There was a meeting of the bank officials on Sunday and I knew it was something serious. Monday morning I didn't use my key to open the bank door, but waited until the cashier arrived. He told me we were closing and that the First National Bank was closing too. I had all my savings in The First National and it threw me for a loop!"

The Punta Gorda State Bank was saved from going under by various citizens, including Barron Collier, who had controlling stock in the bank. He and others brought in "outside" money, paid twenty cents on the dollar and reopened. The other banks never did.

Maude went on to work for the Punta Gorda State Bank for three years, then left to work for Sallie Jones, superintendent of schools, in the courthouse. She retired with Miss Jones in 1953. As a widow, she lived in Charlotte Harbor in the spacious house her husband, Lloyd Mauck, built back in 1927. Her memories of the bank's closing on that fateful Monday morning were still quite vivid in her mind.

Another interesting Depression story comes from Frank Rigell who arrived in Punta Gorda in 1925, right in the middle of the boom. A picture postcard brought him here. Frank, born to Joe and Lizzy Rigell of Slocomb, Alabama, in 1901, was one of seven children. His father owned a combination drygoods-grocery store and also bought and sold cattle. Young Frank had the usual southern childhood and schooling, then went to a business college in Dothan, Alabama, to round out his formal education.

In 1920 some friends of his left for a winter sojourn in Florida, picking oranges. They sent Frank a picture postcard of palm trees silhouetted against a rosy sunset that completely entranced him with the beauty of the Florida evening sky. 'When my friends returned, I asked one of them if it was a touched-up photo. He told me it was the real thing. He himself had seen the sunsets. I decided then and there that if it was that pretty I wanted to go to Florida."

Frank subscribed to a Jacksonville newspaper and studied the help wanted ads. After a few weeks, he found an opening for a payroll clerk and stenographer in a sawmill. Ten days after he answered the ad, he received a wire telling him to report for work immediately, he had a job. The sawmill was in Nocatee, about four or five miles this side of Arcadia. Nocatee was a sawmill and citrus growing town. Finally, Frank was living in Florida.

He liked his new position, worked hard, met a pretty local girl, Rosa Fred, and life was good. Soon the sawmill owners who had lumber yards in Arcadia, Venice, Haines City and Punta Gorda, sent Frank to take charge of the one in Punta Gorda. It was located where Quality Self Storage on Taylor Road is now and was called the West Coast Lumber and Supply Company.

It was the year 1926 when Frank arrived in Punta Gorda—boom time! "There were lots of people here, lots of building going on, lots of real estate changing hands." Frank stayed at the Seminole Hotel, walked to work and ate his meals at any of the four or five restaurants in town that were doing exceedingly well. "When I came here, most of the eating places were jam packed between 11:30 and 1:30 so that people were lined up out into the street. I soon learned to wait 'til about two o'clock to eat. The lumber yard was so busy I worked about eighteen hours a day."

Plans for the Arcade were still on the drawing board. It would be a year before it was finished and a new family in town, The Maxwells, would open their pharmacy there. The post office (to be relocated in the Arcade) was on Marion Avenue where Bill's Tackle Shop is now, across from the Town Clock. Route 41 was still King Street with railroad tracks running along it. Tom Roberts was "tender" of the new bridge (1921) at a salary of $30 a month.

There was a small beach about where the Best Western is and Frank remembers that on Christmas Day people would go swimming there, no matter how cold it was, so they could have their pictures taken to send back north. There was a small pavilion in the area where the townsfolk met to visit, sip drinks and "dance a little bit." Overlooking it all was the imposing Hotel Punta Gorda. Sportsmen, yachtsmen, celebrities and their ladies strolled through the gardens and enjoyed the breathtaking view of the bay from its gracious verandahs. It was a happy, friendly town to which Frank brought his new bride (Rosa Fred of Nocatee) in 1926.

That year the town was at the height of its prosperity; new buildings were going up, stores were doing a land-office business, and real estate transactions were fast and furious. There was a feeling of euphoria in the air throughout the little town. Then the bubble burst.

The Great Depression had already hit the north and now it started its doleful journey southward. In Punta Gorda, Frank recalls, "The Depression hit our little town and hit it hard." Small businesses folded overnight, larger ones took a little longer before they threw in the towel.

As mentioned before all three banks in town closed their doors. Desperate people lined up outside the doors trying to withdraw their money. The story goes that Barron Collier arrived in town with a suitcase full of $5, $10 and $100 bills, handing out this cash to the Punta Gorda State Bank depositors who were clamoring for their funds. By this last minute gesture on Collier's part, disaster at the Punta Gorda State Bank was averted. Depositors got their money back and, not wanting the responsibility of guarding it at home, put it back into the bank. This is one of the many stories of that unfortunate time and, true or not, the fact remains that the Punta Gorda State Bank was the only one to reopen its doors.

The building boom was over, of course, and lumber sales were drastically affected. Frank's employers, owners of four yards, closed all but the one in Punta Gorda. "They told me if I could operate it on my own, I could run it and see how things worked out. Two of the people I had been dealing with told me they'd sell me materials on consignment to help keep me going."

It was an uphill fight, but Frank had always loved the business and his enthusiasm along with faithful customers helped him to keep the yard solvent. After a few years of increasing success, Frank managed to buy the yard, renaming it the Rigell Lumber and Supply Company.

The business did well under Frank's ownership. "It's easier to work hard at something you love" and Frank loved the lumber business. His dream of living in Florida had come true. He had a happy marriage and two daughters, Peggy and Jean. Jean was at one time director of service clubs at Patrick Air Force Base and Peggy married Victor Desguin and had six children who, in turn, presented Frank with six great-grandchildren.

Under doctor's orders, Frank sold the lumber yard in 1957 to A. C. Frizzell and became a man of leisure. Although he and Rosa Fred did a lot of traveling and Frank took up golf, he did find time to be a city councilman from 1960 through 1963.

Frank had a house built on West Palm Avenue in 1963 and the following year he and Rosa Fred and two grandchildren took a long-awaited trip to Hawaii. In 1966 Rosa Fred died and Frank lived alone in the house until 1971 when he married Lou, one of Rosa Fred's closest friends. After all these years, the memory of that fateful day the banks closed is still etched in his memory.

* * *

"Little Doc" Whitehurst was about ten when the Depression hit our town. "Little Doc's" name came about in the following manner. If you can't stand your name, you'll latch onto the first nickname that comes your way. Percy Whitehurst was an example. He was always called "Doc" and when he and his wife, Elsie, had a son and named him Gerald, Gerald became "Little Doc" until his father died, when he became "Doc" and we'll call him that now.

Doc was born in a white frame house on Sullivan Street in the proximity of the Professional Building's parking lot. The house was bulldozed away many years ago, much to Doc's regret. "There was a big field back of our house and daddy always had a large garden growing there. Our chickens used to meet daddy every evening and walk him home from the courthouse. They knew he was fixin' to feed them." The Whitehursts also had a cow they kept tethered in the field right in downtown Punta Gorda!

At the time the Depression hit, Doc's father was an engineer on one of T. C. Crosland's runboats; Crosland owned the West Coast Fish Company. The work was arduous and the hours long; the boats left Punta Gorda at dawn to deliver ice, groceries and supplies to the way stations up and down the bay, laying over that night at the south end of Charlotte Harbor. The next morning they headed back north, stopping at the same icehouses to pick up the fish, weigh them, load them on board and make deliveries at the fish houses in Punta Gorda. For this long and strenuous labor, Doc's father was paid $6 a week!

However, says Doc, "We owned our house, groceries were extremely cheap, our light bill was nothing to speak of and we'd never even heard of air conditioning. When I was a little boy, people didn't run the lights all night, they couldn't. The town plant had a little donkey engine and they'd shut down at 10 o'clock at night." Living was easy at the Whitehurst's comfortable home and $6 went a long way.

"Then came the bad times of the Depression and Roosevelt began the giveaway coupons—I forget the name for them. Once a week you could go downtown and apply for food stamps. Our family was able to get along without them until one night when daddy came home with the news that T. C. Crosland couldn't meet the payroll that week. He told Momma she'd have to go to town and apply for stamps for the groceries. Momma had a proud streak in her and she just plain wouldn't do it. She sent me and Faye instead. We kids went down there and they gave us some flour, potatoes, lard, groceries and milk. We brought it home and Momma started cooking our dinner, standing at the stove, crying. She cried all through dinner. Next week T. C. was able to meet his payroll and we never had to go back again to get free groceries.

"I've thought many times since about the Depression here. Although people had to have groceries and all, I didn't feel too sorry for the people here. How could you starve in Punta Gorda then? The bay was full of fish, you could grow your own food, you could go hunting for meat. I felt for the people in the large cities who had nothing at all except what could be brought to them. You couldn't starve, couldn't even be hungry in Punta Gorda then."

Doc Whitehurst recalls that "not only did no one starve in Punta Gorda during the Depression, but there were some festive times, too. At the height of the bad times, there was the biggest celebration this town has ever seen, before or since! On July 4, 1931, the Barron Collier bridge was dedicated and anybody who was anybody came. They came from Lee County, Polk, DeSoto, Sarasota and even inland counties. The Depression was forgotten for a day; they came by boat, car and by train. On that sweltering 4th of July it was estimated almost 14,000 people swarmed through the Punta Gorda streets!

There were baseball games, fishing contests and a giant fish fry. "There were three huge serving centers along the bayfront in Gilchrist Park. There were lines of people—ten abreast. I was just a little kid in the middle of one of those lines, got overheated, knocked down (by accident) and thought I was going to die in there. Finally some men noticed, small as I was, that I was in trouble and they pulled me out of there. What a press of people that day! There has never been anything in Punta Gorda since to match that happy celebration in the midst of unhappy times!"

* * *

When we discussed the pineapple industry in the area, we described Fabias Perkins' pinery in Solana, on the outskirts of Punta Gorda. Fabias and Susan Perkins had five children, the youngest of whom was Emmett Longwood Perkins. We told of Emmett's taking over the pinery when his father's health began to fail and the subsequent sale of the land upon Fabias' death. As you may recall, Emmett and the rest of the family had moved into Punta Gorda where Emmett went to work as service manager of Jim Goff's Ford Garage.

Meanwhile back in Carmi, Illinois, Emmett's future was about to be decided by a family there, the Erkmans. Carmi, the county seat of White County, Illinois is located thirty-five miles west of Evansville, Indiana, as the crow flies and a glance at a road map shows that you almost have to fly by crow to get there. It's in southern Illinois where the mountains begin to flatten out and where Skillet Fork River runs into the Little Wabash. The area is rich in oil and coal, wheat and soy beans and Martin Erkman called it home. He was very content there, had married a young widow with three little girls and soon had a family of eleven children!

Martin loved the Illinois countryside but his wife, Mary, yearned for sunnier climes, namely Punta Gorda, where one of her brothers lived. Never underestimate the power of a woman. As soon at the older children had settled into lives of their own, Martin, Mary and the four remaining girls pulled up stakes and headed for Punta Gorda. The year was 1925.

The Erkmans bought a house on Virginia Avenue. The two younger girls attended school and the older ones found jobs. Ruth, the oldest, was employed at the *Punta Gorda Herald* as bookkeeper, proofreader and subscription clerk. Martin, an interior decorator, immediately started a project on Amy Holderby McQueen's house. Amy's father, Nathaniel, was an attorney in Carmi and a lifelong friend of Martin. The job had just been completed to Amy's satisfaction when a devastating hurricane hit the town. The violent storm demolished Martin's handiwork; the roof of the house was torn off and the windows blown in. Martin had to start all over again. He went on to other jobs after this but his heart was always in Carmi. His daughter, Ruth's, was not.

Some people meet "across a crowded room." Ruth Erkman and Emmett Perkins caught eyes across Herald Court; the window of her newspaper office overlooked his in Goff's garage. This led to "chance" meetings during the lunch hour. The handsome bachelor and the pretty bookkeeper soon were keeping company. In 1927 Martin issued an ultimatum to his family. "I am going back to Carmi. Those who are going with me be ready to leave the day after high school graduation!" Ruth stayed behind, going to live with her uncle. "I wasn't about to leave Emmett with all those pretty girls in town!"

They were married on Christmas Eve, 1927, and shortly thereafter Ruth left the *Punta Gorda Herald* to work for the insurance agency next door. By then the Great Depression was on and the insurance agency was in trouble and up for grabs. In 1934, Ruth and Emmett took the plunge and bought the business; now it was the Perkins Insurance Agency. Ruth held down the office and Emmett, having left the garage, looked for another job to "keep their heads above water. Times were bad."

Charlotte County at that time had only three school buses, "old wrecks," and Emmett took on the job of keeping them running. One week he would overhaul the bus in Placida, next week on to Bermont and then home to Punta Gorda where he not only serviced the bus but drove it as well. In his spare time, Emmett helped Ruth at the agency, driving with her to visit every home in the county on which they had written a policy. "We knew every house in Charlotte County. 'Course there weren't so many before the war."

The Depression finally came to an end, the Perkins Insurance Agency prospered and the hard times were a thing of the past.

Hard times had come to the Durrance family of Charlotte Harbor along with everybody else, but possibly more forcefully.

Christine Durrance (Donald) belongs to a family steeped in this area's history. Her maternal grandfather, Owen H. Dishong, has a Florida town named for him—Owens—and he also was a sheriff of this county when it was part of Manatee County. Her paternal grandfather, Francis M. Durrance, a United States customs officer, was the first Methodist minister in Punta Gorda. Durrance Street was named in his honor.

Christine "Pat" was born in Wauchula, Florida, in 1923, second child of Cleveland and May Dishong Durrance. Her father had a successful drygoods store there, but moved to Punta Gorda when Pat was two years old. The land boom was on and he went into the real estate business here. He bought a spacious home on the river in Charlotte Harbor. That home, on Melbourne Street, was a restaurant for many years. Pat and her sister, Alla May, had a lively childhood growing up in the big house on the water.

When the Depression came, the real estate business was one of the first to feel it. Cleveland Durrance was fortunate enough to find another line of work. He became a bank receiver and there were lots of banks to receive in those difficult times. The family seemed to be weathering the storm well and then disaster struck. Cleveland Durrance was stricken with a heart attack and died. It was the depth of the Depression, 1935, when May Durrance was left a widow with two young girls to raise. Pat, the youngest, was only twelve and remembers the crisis. "Some friends talked Momma into opening a real estate office; she was the first woman real estate broker in Charlotte County."

To supplement her income, May decided to rent rooms to winter visitors. A big sign went up, "Rooms to Rent—May has it!" Her daughters could never pin their mother down as to what that meant! Both girls attended Charlotte High. Pat had skipped a grade in the Charlotte Harbor School, so they waited together every morning for the school bus by the three oak trees that stood where the Harbor Inn is now. Since their mother was busy with the real estate office, the girls showed and rented the rooms. Pat feels it was a good experience. She enjoyed talking with the Yankee visitors and hearing about the world outside little Charlotte Harbor and Punta Gorda.

Being the youngest pupil in the ninth grade, Pat came in for some friendly teasing. One "tormentor" was Robert Donald, several grades ahead of Pat. He delighted in pulling her long curls. "He made me mad as the devil, but that's when I first noticed him." Noticing turned to dating and in time the two were "going steady." Since Pat was so young the dates were mainly at church affairs. A favorite spot was the Seminole Pharmacy for ice cream or a cherry smash.

Durrance Realty was doing well and the mother, May, had become a well-known figure around town, always fashionably dressed and always wearing a big pinwheel hat. "She had them in every color to match her outfits."

After graduation from high school at sixteen, Pat spent two years at Florida Southern College, then came home to marry Robert. Theirs was a festive wedding in the house by the river, Reverend Sutley officiating. The newlyweds settled in Maryland where Robert worked as a machinist in the U.S. Navy Yard; Pat worked for the IRS and the U.S. Public Health Service, but left the business world when a daughter, Christine, was born. In 1945 Robert suggested to Pat that they return to Punta Gorda and she was on the phone to her mother in a matter of minutes. The Maryland house was put up for sale and within two weeks the Donalds headed south.

Robert bought a house on Trabue Avenue and became the Trailways agent at its original location across from the old hotel. Pat became a working partner in her mother's real estate business. "It was now Durrance and Donald."

In 1943 a son, Robert L., was born and the family was complete. Energetic Pat mixed maternal duties with the real estate business and, as if that weren't enough, opened the first travel agency in the county! Things went smoothly for the Donalds until 1964 when their luck ran out. Pat was forced to close Durrance and Donald due to her mother's ill health and Robert developed heart trouble.

In 1965, Robert died at age of forty-five, leaving Pat in the same situation as her mother thirty years earlier. Seeking security, she sold the travel agency and went to work for the Charlotte County Health Department. Starting as a secretary, she worked her way to business manager and retired after working twenty years with the department.

Strong Families and Strong Women

It was long before the Great Depression, way back in the early 1900s, that Elsie Johnson Daughtry found herself thrust out into the world to make a living for herself and her children.

Her parents, Nettie and Sumner Johnson, had come here from Fort Ogden around 1910. They settled in Charlotte Harbor on what was to become Melbourne Street, but what was then just a nameless sandy road along the river. There were four children in the family. Sumner was a boat builder.

Elsie, born in 1900, grew up swimming in the bay, fishing off the dock "right out from my house," playing Hail Over and Stick Frog. She remembers her skirts were halfway between knee and ankle— "hot to wear in the summer but I got used to it." There was no bridge to Punta Gorda; the mail boat carried passengers for fifty cents. Life was simple and hard work was expected of one and all.

The Arcadia courthouse was the site of Elsie's marriage to John Daughtry, a field foreman for an orange crew. They settled in Fort Ogden and started a family: three girls, Dolores, Violet and Christine. John didn't live to see his girls grow up. In 1924 medicine was not an exact science and John died of what was diagnosed as "either pleurisy or a heart attack." The young father died five days before his oldest daughter's fourth birthday.

Elsie was left a young widow with three children to raise, the young-est, Christine, only four months! When asked how she managed, Elsie shrugged and said, "I did what young folk today wouldn't do. I took the three little ones and I went out in the fields and hoed orange trees for $1 a day. They didn't plant orange trees close together like they do now. They had to be eight feet apart. What they couldn't get under with a plow, I hoed out." While Elsie worked, the little girls stayed on a quilt under a tree. "Folks said, 'You're going to kill those young'uns,' but nobody offered to help." Somehow the youngsters and Elsie survived and eventually her widowed father persuaded her to pack up the children and come home to Charlotte Harbor.

Her father was ailing and Elsie took on even more responsibilities. To help make ends meet, she took in washing. "I went and picked up the dirty clothes, washed and ironed them and carried them back for $1.50." On her numerous "laundry trips" Elsie met a young man, Harold Matheson, who worked at a filling station. Despite all her obligations, romance managed to flourish and in 1927 Harold and Elsie were married. Soon there were four more children: Ida Mae, Clara, Harold and Ruth.

Lest we think that Elsie never did anything but work, work, work; her daughter Christine recalls, "Momma loved to dance and wore out a pair of dancing shoes every five or six weeks!" At this writing, Elsie was retired and a living example of how a brave young woman (She was only twenty-four when her husband died.) held her little brood together through sheer grit and determination before the days of organizations geared to help in such a situation.

In the days when a woman's place was in the home, Jean Cleveland, proved the exception to the rule. She was able to run a household and venture out into the business world at the same time.

This lady met life head-on with a droll sense of humor that seemed to lift her over the rough spots and allowed her to enjoy to the utmost whatever life had to offer. Jean was born in Brooksville, Florida, in 1891. Her father, Ulysses Simpson Whiteaker, and mother, Nora, came south from Missouri in the late 1800s and stayed in Brooksville long enough for Jean to be born. They then returned briefly to Missouri and in 1906, U. S. Whiteaker brought his family back to Florida and settled in Punta Gorda.

U. S. Whiteaker was a man of varied interests, like his grandson and namesake, U. S. Cleveland. He was a minister, cigar manufacturer, school teacher and farmer—a man for all seasons. The cigar manufacturing business proved to be not very lucrative and the monetary reward for spreading the gospel was meager, to say the least. His roles as a farmer and teacher were what put the bread on the table for the Whiteakers.

His daughter, Jean, was fifteen years old when the family moved to Punta Gorda and one of her earliest memories is of going through the Hotel Punta Gorda on a quiet Sunday afternoon. "The hotel was closed for the summer and we could take our time seeing everything. It was such a lovely spacious hotel with a definite air of elegance about it. Later, I went to school banquets and dances there."

A friend of Jean's lived in Boca Grande and, during a visit there, Jean met a dashing young man, Cleve Henry Cleveland, who was an engineer on a pilot boat. Boca Grande was a busy shipping center at that time and cargo from all over the world was delivered there. The pilot boat met the incoming vessels and steered them through the pass into the harbor.

Love, too, will find a way and Cleve managed to use the pilot boat on trips to the mainland where his family lived. It was also an excellent excuse to see Jean. The romance stayed on a steady course and Cleve and Jean were married in 1914 and set up housekeeping in Boca Grande down by the docks, handy for Cleve's new job as stevedore for the phosphate company. Three of their four sons were born in Boca Grande: Cleve Gerald, William Alan and Ulysses Samuel. In 1921 Gerald became of school age and, since the nearest school was more than two miles away—there were no school buses then—the family moved to Punta Gorda.

Cleve went to work for the city as an electrician and, when Punta Gorda sold their "lights" to the Florida Power and Light Company, Cleve went to work for them. Meanwhile, Jean wasn't exactly idle herself. Besides raising the youngsters and keeping the home fires burning, she taught the second grade at the Taylor Street School—forty-four kids in a class! In 1923 Jean gave up teaching to become a mother for the fourth time, another son, Max.

The four Cleveland boys were growing up and when U. S.'s youngest brother, Max had reached the ripe old age of one and a half, mother Jean went to work at city hall as deputy clerk. Jean's sister-in-law was at home and looked after the youngsters while Jean was at work.

The job at city hall was an intricate one, entailing the compiling of the tax roll, issuing licenses, keeping the books for the water department and the ever-expanding municipal trailer park. It kept Jean on her toes, juggling the many responsibilities of a deputy clerk. There was only one office from which everything evolved; now, of course, there are many, all computerized. Jean spent thirty-one years at city hall, the last eight as the first female city clerk in Punta Gorda.

After working for Florida Power and Light for fifteen years, Cleve went to work for himself, operating an electrical repair business out of the family home on Gill Street. He knew just about everybody in town after reading meters all those years and his electrical expertise became legend. His business expanded through word-of-mouth advertising and it became common knowledge around Punta Gorda that "there's nothing Cleve can't fix."

After World War I, the Essex and the Star, Ford's flivver and the Moon were fast replacing earlier horseless carriages. It became more dangerous to drive or walk on the streets of Punta Gorda in the 1920s and '30s. No driver's license was required in those days; anybody who owned or had access to an automobile was free to navigate the streets. So when Cleve's new Willys Baby Overland was delivered downtown, he didn't hesitate to call Jean to come down and drive it home. It didn't matter that she had never driven before! Jean, never one to resist a challenge, was willing. Cleve had her climb up on the fire engine at city hall so he could show her how a gearshift worked. A short lesson and then Jean took off on her "solo" trip home.

She managed to shift beautifully from first to second and was thoroughly enjoying herself. Negotiating third gear turned out to be a different matter all together. Hearing the grinding of gears, Olive Curry looked out her window and saw Jean's predicament. A more seasoned driver, Olive dashed across the yard, hopped onto the runningboard of the balking automobile, maneuvered the gearshift lever into third while Jean de-clutched and hopped off. The day and the car had been saved. Jean did manage to get the brake on and the engine turned off as she sailed into the driveway at 509 Gill Street.

This adventure brings to mind a story Faye Whitehurst Mobley Austin told about her mother's driving. When Faye was growing up in

Punta Gorda, the "main drag" was from city hall east to where the post office is now, and traffic, though light, could prove exciting. At the time of this incident, Faye's mother, Elsie, was a new and extremely nervous driver. Once behind the wheel she had a tendency to become erratic and excitable. One day, as she was driving downtown, a fire engine pulled up behind her, clanging its bell . Volunteer firemen were rushing out of the stores into the street to hop on the passing fire truck. This all added to the confusion.

Elsie panicked and, just as Arthur Goff darted out to join his fellow volunteers, she stepped on the gas instead of the brake, knocking him flat! Astounded by what she had done, Elsie stopped the car by putting on the brake just as a front wheel rolled up on his chest. Fortunately, cars were light in those days. When Deputy Lewis ran over to the now ashen-faced and trembling Elsie he pleaded with her to "release your brake so we can get Arthur off the street." No serious harm had been done and Arthur gratefully walked away.

After this initial shock, Elsie recovered and undaunted, continued to drive for many months until she lost an argument with a locomotive. She survived this encounter but it put an end to her driving.

Mary Ellen Glover Manning's childhood, the Glover Ships Chandlery, and Manning's hardware store were mentioned in an earlier chapter. Her youngest child, Larry, had the distinction of being the first baby born at the Charlotte Hospital on August 30, 1947. When he was old enough, Mary Ellen decided to go to work. In 1958 she found employment in the property appraiser's office, working for Claude Roberts and later, Oliver Lowe.

In the eighteen years she worked there, a lot of property was appraised as Punta Gorda grew from a small town to the busy community it is today. In 1958, Belle Quednau's "old crabbing grounds" were just beginning to be developed into sprawling Punta Gorda Isles. Mary Ellen watched even more growth across the river when General Development Corp. exploded into Port Charlotte. In 1978, Mary Ellen Manning retired and lived in the big house her father built when she was ten years old. Although Joe passed away in 1980, her children all lived in the state and she had a host of friends nearby. She was quoted as saying, "I'm happy here and wouldn't live anywhere else in the world!"

Another Punta Gorda housewife who made the plunge into a "man's world," was Areta Yeager. Ed and Areta had built a large home on East McKenzie but lost it during the depression and moved into what Areta jokingly called "the little shack" on Marion Avenue. "The little shack" is a gem of a house now in the heart of downtown Punta Gorda and Areta's daughter and her husband, Areta and Robert Futch live there today. The house looks as if it should be on a quiet country lane, but, instead is adjacent to a business block to the east and the old Punta Gorda Arcade to the west. Past its front door flows the traffic of U.S. 17 from Arcadia and points north and east, and across Marion Avenue is the very busy Punta Gorda post office.

E. B. Yeager was county tax collector from 1932 to 1952 when he died in office. His wife, Areta, took over the reins until 1972. Thus the office of county tax collector stayed forty years under the name Yeager!

In a previous chapter we described the Morgan mansion built for Martha Susanna Morgan in 1911. Her granddaughter, Mattie Mae McDaniel (Hughes), really broke the barrier for women in the masculine-dominated cattle industry.

Mattie Mae was born at home in 1919 on King Street where the Texaco Station is located. "It was a dirt road and there were two big brown, two-story houses side by side. I was born in one of them and Momma had quite a time having me. Dr. McQueen was having trouble delivering me so Daddy got in his Model T and drove to Arcadia to get another doctor to help him. Between the two of them they got me born."

Of her early childhood in Punta Gorda Mattie Mae remembers best her Uncle Jess with deep affection. "He was something special. He liked to hunt and fish and when I was about five, he brought me a baby fox with a silver collar. We used to keep it tied to the front porch. One day somebody came along and stole it—collar and all.

"Uncle Jess had two dogs, Bounce and Bull. When he left to out to the grove, those old dogs would go around the house looking for him. When they couldn't find him, we'd see them trotting down the road to the grove. There wasn't much traffic on Taylor Road then. If he wasn't there, we'd soon see them ambling back to town."

Mattie Mae was a tomboy. When other little girls were playing with dolls, Mattie Mae was trading pocket knives, toad frogs and whatnots in school. "I loved horses and I got Daddy to take me around to the horse auctions. I wanted a horse so badly. I admired the western cowboys in the moves because they rode horses and were the kings of everything they surveyed. I wanted to be a cowboy, but I couldn't because I was a damn female. Couldn't go away from home 'cause Momma said, 'Girls don't do things like that.' I rebelled. I hated it. It's a wonder I didn't run away from home."

However, the little girl was very much in awe of one female who was quite a lady, her Great Aunt Lizzy (Elizabeth Cushing). "She was Grandma Morgan's oldest sister and had married a New York millionaire. She lived right across from the courthouse. She was the sweetest person I have ever known in my whole life. She usually wore a dark dress with starched lacy cuffs and a lace collar that came around her neck real tight. Her dress came down to about three inches above her ankles and she wore highbutton black shoes.

"She had the prettiest eyes. They were the color of violets and she wore her hair parted in the middle and pulled back. When she talked she had the softest voice, but you could hear her plainly and she'd sit with her hands folded quietly in her lap. When I went over to her, she'd lean down, kiss me and say, 'Sit down, child.' Then she'd talk to Momma. I was so fascinated that I'd just sit and stare at her."

When Mattie Mae was fourteen, her grandfather McDaniel had a stroke and Howard McDaniel, his wife, Frances, and their daughter moved to Woodville to help out, as families did in those days. There was no school in town and Frances didn't want her young daughter traveling to Tallahassee so Mattie Mae had no schooling for two years.

"I stayed up there and hunted in the hummock, brought rabbits and squirrels home to eat. Daddy couldn't get his plumber's license for six months with our move to another county and we had to have food. I cleared new ground around the hummock with the black men and worked all day long for fifty cents." Mattie Mae stood in line to get her precious fifty cents, but was given half a can of blackstrap molasses instead for working a full day in the field. Child labor laws weren't strictly enforced then.

Up on Woodville when fifteen-year old Mattie Mae wasn't hunting on the hummock or working in the fields for a half can of blackstrap molasses, she also sawed wood with a handsome young man, her first love. "We'd cut it with an old crosscut saw, split it, load up a wagon and mule, haul it and sell it for $1.50 a cord."

Back home in Punta Gorda, Mattie Mae's Aunt Maude had her hands full running the huge Morgan house and felt it would be a good thing for her young niece to get back to school, so Mattie Mae tearfully told her boyfriend good-bye and returned to Punta Gorda.

Every morning, after helping her Aunt Maude with the household chores, Mattie Mae trudged off to Charlotte High School. She remembers how hot and thirsty she would be and how she used to stop at the old artesian well in town and drink her fill.

After Grandpa McDaniel's death, Mattie Mae's parents came home to Punta Gorda. "We lived in what was then known as the old Vogler place next door to Grandma's grove. Tosie Hindman lives on that piece of land now. Daddy rented an old barn where the *Herald News* building is now and opened his own plumbing business."

When Mattie Mae graduated from Charlotte High, she had read everything they had in the library and wanted to be an advertising copy-writer, but by that time, "Momma was sick and I had to stay home." She fell back on her trading expertise (toad frogs and jackknives in school) and soon was in the cattle business. Mrs. A. C. Frizzell took an interest in the hard-working girl and gave her the use of some land around Jones Loop Road for grazing her cows. "I saved my lunch money and became a horse and cow trader, traded all over Florida—auctions in Wauchula, Live Oak, Sarasota and Bradenton—traded until I got up to sixty-four head of cattle!"

Mattie Mae's rugged way of life finally took its toll. When she was twenty-four, she became seriously ill with pneumonia and was hospitalized in Arcadia, but Mattie Mae couldn't be kept down for long. Feeling that her hospital stay wasn't doing her that much good, she decided to make an "illegal" departure.

"One day a fellow who worked for my daddy came by to see how I was. I told him I was going home and he was going to take me. 'Miss Mattie, you can't leave without checking out.' I said, 'Just be quiet and do what I say. Get my clothes out of the closet, shut the door, go down the hall and get a wheelchair.' By the time he got back I had somehow, sick as I was, yanked my clothes on and was ready to go. He lifted me into the chair, pushed me to the back service elevator, rolled me out the back door of that hospital and plunked me down in his truck."

"I passed out twice on the way home, that's how sick I was. He stopped in town at Mobley's and got me a cherry coke. I'll never forget that. It revived me a little bit. When we got home, Momma was so glad to see me. She had no way of getting to Arcadia. She fixed me up with a Vicks salve poultice, lit our old oil stove and had me stick my head in the oven. The heat and the salve did the trick."

Mattie Mae finished her convalescence at her Grandma Morgan's house in town and decided to sell off her cattle since she wasn't well enough to take care of them. "After I sold the cattle and paid my hospital bill, I had only $1,600 left to show for four years of hard work and I mean hard work—building fences, screw-worming calves, tending the cows and pulling calves. Sixteen hundred dollars comes to $400 a year, about $1.50 a day.

Despite Frances McDaniel's home remedy of poultice and oven heat for her daughter's pneumonia, Mattie Mae's recovery was slow and she spent a year in bed at her grandmother's house in town. Miss Sallie Jones, the well-known teacher and a family friend, became concerned about the young girl's health.

"Miss Sallie took me in her car all the way to Tampa to see a specialist. He told me my heart and lungs had suffered damage from the pneumonia and he wanted me to have complete rest. Told me to sit in a chair in the sun, fish, do what I liked to do but no hard work."

Mattie Mae took it easy as long as she could stand it, then, feeling better, she started working in Mrs. Handlon's bakery in town and, later on, in the Tamiami Bar also owned by Mrs. Handlon. As she regained her strength, she worried about her mother. "Mama wasn't well and at home out at the creek by herself. Daddy was there but gone all day."

Mattie Mae told Mrs. Handlon she was going to have to find a job that paid more so she could move her mother to town. An ad in the local paper for a two-story apartment house with a shop downstairs had caught her eye but she didn't have enough money. Mrs. Handlon admired Mattie Mae; the girl had spunk and she was a hard worker. Mrs. Handlon didn't want to lose her so she loaned Mattie Mae enough to buy the place. The three apartments upstairs were rented and Mattie Mae converted the large area downstairs into a plumbing shop for her father and a two-bedroom apartment for the family living quarters.

Mattie Mae was also helping Aunt Maude take care of her ailing grandmother. Working long hours at the bar just became too much. She borrowed from the bank, paid back Mrs. Handlon and left the Tamiami Bar. Her income from several paper routes, delivering telegrams and handing out pamphlets for the B&B plus the revenue from the apartments and her father's plumbing business kept the family afloat.

When Mattie Mae's mother wished she had room for a garden, Mattie Mae bought the lot next door. Soon Frances was happily planting flowers. This was Mattie Mae's first taste of acquiring land and she liked it. Reverting to her horse trading days, she began buying old houses, sometimes moving them to other lots and fixing them up to rent. Eventually she "somehow" accumulated ten to twelve houses.

One of the houses she moved was already rented by James J. Hughes who worked for the Winter Garden Ornamental Nursery in Punta Gorda. She was moving the house to McKenzie and Lemon Streets right across from the nursery so Jimmy ended up closer to his work and didn't even have to move!

This particular business transaction played an important part in Mattie Mae's future. Jimmy began courting her while paying his paper bill and rent. Quite often he'd bring along his three sons by a previous marriage. Mattie Mae became not only a bride, but an instant mother when she was married in Arcadia with two cowboys (Who else?) as witnesses.

Mattie Mae lived "out in the creek" (Burnt Store Road) with her children by Jimmy—Martha and Joe—and grandchildren nearby. She had "fifty or sixty" head of cattle at the time she was interviewed for this book. At that time she said, "In fact there are two cows that have had calves since I've been out there; haven't had time to congratulate them."

Mattie Mae lugged bales of hay to feed her cattle, did most of the repairs, painted her rented houses and anything else that needed doing around the place. She fought her way with grit and determination; and is a reminder of the pioneer stock that founded old Punta Gorda.

* * *

Then there's Tosie Quednau Hindman with enough energy and enthusiasm for two women! Young Cap'n Fred and Belle Quednau had an only child, a spunky little girl who, as soon as she could talk, waddled around on her baby legs, demanding "toas, toas"—her favorite food. Thus Henrietta M. Quednau became forever "Tosie."

Tosie spent most of her early years aboard her daddy's boat. Cap'n Fred was the youngest captain sailing the "islands run" and he liked to have his wife and daughter with him. Belle enjoyed the ever-changing scenery and the more than comfortable living accommodations, but looking after an adventurous energetic little girl on board ship was something else again!

For example, one day Cap'n Fred was docking at Useppa Island when a deck hand yelled, "Man overboard." Fred quickly reversed engines in time to keep Tosie from being crushed between the boat and the dock. Emulating her older cousins who had already jumped to the pier from the moving boat, Tosie had missed connections and ended up in the drink!

Over the years Tosie became a natural sailor and no more mishaps occurred, but she was approaching school age and some changes had to be made. Belle and Tosie moved back to town to the more staid life of landlubbers while Fred sailed alone. This arrangement didn't last long. Fred was a family man at heart, a sailor second. He returned to the land and his little family. Being a natural-born cook, he ventured into the restaurant business, opening Fred's Quick Lunch on Marion Avenue. It was an immediate success. Later on, Fred entered the political arena, first as councilman, then becoming mayor of Punta Gorda in the '30s and sheriff of Charlotte County after that.

In the meantime, Tosie was growing up and having a wonderful time. There were Girl Scout camp outs down near the river and scavenger hunts. There were picnics and fish fries, swimming parties and dances.

A. C. Frizzell, the land and cattle baron who owned thousands of acres of what is now Port Charlotte, had two nephews, Joyce and Jack Hindman. The two boys came to live with him on his ranch in Murdock when they were in their early teens. While attending Charlotte

High School, it was inevitable that Jack should meet the irrepressible Tosie Quednau.

Tosie and Jack were married ten months after Pearl Harbor. The marriage license was unique in that the same name, Henry Quednau, appears as best man on both Tosie's and her parents' marriage certificates. The names are the same, but the signatures are different—they are those of father and son.

After only six weeks of marriage, Jack went into the Marine Corps and he and his young bride were separated for the duration of the war. Tosie kept herself busy helping Lois Peeples at the Peeples' IGA grocery store because Vasco was overseas, too. The two women had to learn how to butcher meat. Deputy Sheriff Travis Parnell, came over when he was off duty to give them lessons on "breaking down a quarter of beef." So now our Tosie was an amateur butcher among other things. She also worked as a cashier for Dick Lawhorne of "Lawhorne's Food Palace."

When the war was over, Jack Hindman ran a service station for a while before going to work as a ranch foreman for his uncle, A. C. Frizzell. The young couple settled in on the Frizzell ranch, setting up housekeeping in quarters at the rear of the Murdock Mercantile Store. As mentioned earlier, Frizzell's Mercantile Store handled just about everything, including the United States mail. Tosie became postmistress and also helped in the store.

Tosie was one busy lady, since by now she and Jack had a son, Arthur "Bunk" Ray. When Tosie wasn't carrying the mail sacks to and from the depot, or waiting on the postal customers and store patrons, she was riding herd on Bunk who roared around the premises on his little walker. "Bunk could scoot around that store faster than that old train could come down that old railroad track!"

Bunk's brother, Freddie, was born in 1947 and the family moved back to Punta Gorda in the late '50s. While Jack commuted to Murdock and his job on the ranch, and with the boys now in school, Tosie put Travis Parnell's past teaching to work and became a meat cutter for the U-Save Market in Punta Gorda.

Tosie Hindman loves people, especially children, so it was only natural that when she was offered a job driving a school bus, she would put down her butcher knife at the U-Save and take up the wheel. Her route was Punta Gorda Isles, Harbour Heights and Port Charlotte. She had more than the usual share of unforgettable moments.

One sunny morning, Tosie picked up a first grade pupil, a boy who was balancing three coffee cans along with his books. Something for Show and Tell, thinks Tosie. Minutes later, driving down Olympia Avenue, pandemonium broke out with enough hollering and screaming to take the roof off the bus! Slowing down and adjusting the rear view mirror, Tosie saw a small army of fiddler crabs sidling down the aisle. That little first-grader had brought on board coffee cans full of the scuttling creatures and turned them loose.

Tosie drove very slowly and very carefully to school, cautioning the girls, in particular. "Just pick your feet up off the floor. They won't nip you if you don't bother them." Arriving at school, the children, now safely off and the bus relatively quiet, Tosie cornered the culprit.

"Whatever made you turn those fiddlers loose?" asked Tosie. He reared back on his little legs, looked up at her with wide innocent eyes and blurted out, "It's none of your damn business!" A first grader, no less! The children did love Tosie however and when she started politicking, they were an invaluable asset.

In 1961, A. C. Frizzell died and Jack went to work for the Gulf American Land Corporation in Cape Coral. He worked there until ill health caused his early retirement in 1967. Meanwhile Tosie decided to run for supervisor of elections when the venerable Mrs. Lily King finally retired. "Miss Lily was the sweetest little old lady and I would never have run against her."

Tosie was elected in 1964 and on her last bus drive, the children were in tears. One youngster spoke for all of them when he said, "We wouldn't have asked our mommies and daddies to vote for you if we'd known it meant you weren't going to drive the bus anymore." The kids also got up a petition and presented it to the powers-that-be, asking to have Tosie back. "She's the best hot-rod driver we ever had."

Tosie was supervisor of elections for many years, loved her job and the people she served until she retired. She told me, "So few citizens of this wonderful country of ours go to the polls." She had a motto hanging on the wall of her office that declared DON'T VOTE—DON'T BITCH.

Tosie is sincere in her love affair with the human race and there is not an affected bone in her body. It's a trite phrase, but they did break the mold when they made Tosie Quednau Hindman.

These are but a few of the many women of this area who ventured out into the business world when it was not *de rigueur* and were successful.

Number, Please

It was the year 1923 when Robert C. Bonnell, his wife, Annie, and their baby daughter, Omar, arrived in Punta Gorda. Robert had come here to set up the first telephone office, which was upstairs over John Hathaway's law office on Marion Avenue. Robert's position was general manager which meant, in those days, that he assembled telephones, installed them, kept up the maintenance of the switchboard, climbed the poles for repair and, with his wife, Annie, stuffed envelopes and mailed the bills.

Their baby daughter, Omar, was only four months old so Annie, who was one of the operators, brought her crib to the office and little Omar slept to the lullaby of "Number, please." The other original operators were Miss Minnie Dampier and Mrs. Franabelle Hurd. The telephone office closed at ten P.M. until the following morning at eight. Eventually, the switchboard was equipped with a strident night bell, a cot was moved in and Annie became the first night operator.

Growing up in such close proximity to the telephone office, little Omar "learned her numbers on the switchboard" and finally cajoled her mother into letting her work it. Unbeknownst to her father, when Omar was just in the fourth grade she was "filling in" on the switchboard on weekends! This well-kept secret was out when her father ran into Dan Gibbons sitting on a bench by the Seminole Pharmacy. The conversation went something like this. Gibbons: "Bonnell, I want to know who that new operator is." "Don't have a new one." "Yes, you do. She has the sweetest little voice and she never fails to say thank you." Robert put two and two together and managed to "surprise" Omar at work. Young as she was, the little girl was more than efficient at the switchboard; she had had years of exposure to it. Her dad finally gave his seal of approval to adding another part-time operator to his staff.

In spite of all the various jobs he performed as general manager of the telephone office, Robert's salary was only $130 a month. Annie decided she would add to the family income by opening a drygoods store. The store was originally in the Arcade and for years the Punta Gorda Drygoods Store and Bonnell's Department Store were the only stores of their kind in Punta Gorda. "Daddy still ran the telephone office and came to the store at nights to help mother."

The store was a success and soon outgrew its spot in the Arcade, moving twice more. The last move was on Thanksgiving Day of 1948, a day Omar remembers only too well. First of all, she and her husband, Cecil Keen, had only been married a short time and were barely settled themselves. Secondly, it was a typical Punta Gorda family-type maneuver. Robert and Annie moved Bonnell's Department Store by simply rolling the dress racks down the street to the new location.

Cecil and Omar survived the Thanksgiving trek and went on to raise a family of two girls, Peggy and Lisa. They made their home on Ann Street in a cozy house nestled back among the trees.

Another "telephone girl" was a longtime resident of Punta Gorda and Cleveland, although she didn't join the ranks until 1943. Her memories of early Punta Gorda are too good to miss.

Use your imagination. There is no Punta Gorda Mall downtown, no Publix or Eckerd's, but instead, there stands a luxurious hotel with sweeping verandahs and exotic flowers lining a white shell driveway. Across the street there is no Dean's South of the Border Restaurant. Instead, there is a wooden railroad depot and Captain Allen's two-story rooming house. Behind this is Glover's Marine Hardware Store, handy to the fishing docks and the railroad that juts out into the river. That's the way it was when Elizabeth Bingley came here as a young girl of eleven in 1921.

Elizabeth and her mother settled in Cleveland in the Iverson House right on the waterfront. Elizabeth's sister, Ethel, lived nearby with her husband, Andrew Cleveland, who ran a grocery store and was postmaster and express agent of Cleveland. Elizabeth went to the Taylor Street School in Punta Gorda and was a junior when the new Charlotte

High School opened in 1926. She left school when she was a senior to marry a former classmate, Charles Willis.

Charles was born in Charlotte Harbor in 1909. His father, Jim, and mother, Mary (Dampier), came here from a fishing island off the coast of North Carolina. When Charles was in the fifth grade, the family moved to Goldstein Street in Punta Gorda and he attended the Taylor Street School where he met Elizabeth Bingley. Charles was soon enamored with Elizabeth but not with the academic life (although he had a favorite teacher, Mrs. Esther Jordan McCullough) and he left school in 1926.

Charles joined his young friends who were working on the docks, loading fish into the waiting railroad cars. He also caddied at the big hotel's golf course which later became the Punta Gorda Country Club. When he reached the august age of fifteen, he began to work with his father as a fishing guide at Useppa.

In 1927 Charles and Elizabeth were married and he went to work for Barron Collier at his shipyard in Punta Blanco. The newlyweds lived on the island in a community of "Collier people" until the shipyard closed in 1931. Charles then became an engineer at the power plant at Useppa and the family moved to Bokeelia. In 1932, Florida Power and Light offered him a job as diesel engineer in Lake City and the family moved again and stayed until 1942 when Charles was transferred to his old hometown, Punta Gorda.

During the war years, Elizabeth went to work for the first time in her life, first at the A&P, then in 1943 she joined the telephone company as an operator. Both Charles and Elizabeth retired in the early '70s, and settled in a charming little house on Goldstein Street next door to the original family home.

Edna Earl Smith Poppell, the "Smiling Iceman's" daughter, went to work for the Intercounty Telephone Company after graduating from Charlotte High. She would walk to work every day past the Princess Hotel where Clayton Poppell was a guest. Introductions were finally made and a romance began. You might say the telephone company was responsible for that wedding!

Edna Earl Poppell went back to work after her marriage; her close friends, Audrey Taylor and Jane Weeks, worked there, too. When the telephone company moved the Punta Gorda "girls" to Fort Myers, Edna Earl stayed put, happily pregnant with their first and only child, Sherra Lee. Jane Weeks married Gene Watson and left work when their daughter, Sandra Jean, was born.

Byrdia "Byrd" Strickland Conover Krotine was another local telephone girl, arriving in Punta Gorda by way of Fort Myers. She was only four years old when she hopped off the train in Fort Myers.

The year was 1922 and Florida was in the midst of a boom; land was good as gold and people arrived in droves to join the gold rush. Cornelius Strickland, a young industrious farmer from Bainbridge, Georgia, had come to Fort Myers the year before and was now nervously pacing at the station awaiting the arrival of his wife, Nellie, and their seven children, one a babe-in-arms. His young wife had not been happy to leave family and friends in Georgia and Neal was anxious for her first impression of their new home to be a good one. It was. As tired as Nellie was after twenty-four hours of traveling with six children and a baby, her eyes opened wide as they drove down McGregor Boulevard to the sight of exotic flowers, bougainvilleas and red hibiscus. The royal palms dispelled all doubt about the family's move!

There was a rude awakening after a week of readjustment. It was May, the rainy season, the mosquitoes were thriving and the smell of sulfur in the air was a new and unpleasant experience. There was no such thing as city water and people either dug wells (hence the aroma of sulfur) or used cisterns to catch the rain. For a while Nellie yearned to go back to Georgia—lovely flowers or not—but she stayed and Neal soon moved his family upriver to Tice.

Byrd spent most of her childhood on the grove in Tice, graduated from high school at the early age of sixteen and that same year became the bride of Haywood Conover. So it was as a very young bride that Byrd arrived in Punta Gorda. Haywood managed the A&P and Byrd remembers, "Punta Gorda was just a sleepy little town then, that never grew. Only Marion Avenue was busy and the fish docks and groves. Of course, we had the big hotel; a lot of people depended on it for their livelihood. It was a beautiful old thing."

Byrd's new friends, like the Wilkinson and Guthrie girls, were still in school, but she joined the Woman's Club and the Garden Club. On

Thursdays she drove her Model A around the county, the twin Mack boys on the running board, delivering handbills for the store.

The town was quiet, but local boys found things to do, such as on Halloween driving a cow up the wooden stairs of the Taylor Street School; the auditorium was never the same. Some of these practical jokers caught an unusually large jewfish in the harbor, painted it multicolored and added a tusk and horns. They delighted in luring gullible tourists to the back of the store to see what exotic fish could be caught in these waters!

In spite of the sleepy town atmosphere, there was a lively social life. There were good times at the annual Sadie Hawkins Day Dance held in the Woman's Club building. "Haywood won first prize once as Hairless Joe, a character out of the Li'l Abner comic strip. There were dinner parties and bridge, but with no children as yet, time began to lie heavily on Byrd's hands.

Soon there wasn't time enough; Byrd was managing the dining room at the Eagle's Nest and also working as a relief telephone operator in the Punta Gorda office. There was a cot for the all-night operator and a strident night bell. Nevertheless, Byrd remarks, "I was a sound sleeper, so I slept with the headphones on my ears! When it buzzed, I'd jump up, run to the switchboard, plug myself in and say, 'number please'."

When the war came, Haywood Conover was among the first to enlist and, as luck would have it, his first station was crash boat duty at Fort Myers Beach! Haywood and Byrd rented their home on Carmalita Street and moved to Fort Myers where Byrd worked for the telephone office there. When Haywood went overseas to India, Byrd went to work at Buckingham Air Force Base in the Signal Center and remained there throughout the war.

When the war was over, the Conovers moved back to Punta Gorda. Haywood's old job at the A&P was waiting for him and the couple settled down to raise a family. Jennifer was born in 1948 and Holly, twenty-one months later. Byrd now had her hands full running the house and looking after two lively little girls.

When the girls started school, Byrd went back to work, this time with the First National Bank. A few years later Haywood left the A&P

and bought the only laundry in town, originally owned by Mac MacGibbon. He also took over the bottled gas franchise that went with it. Energetic Byrd added a pottery shop in the back and a small orchid hothouse.

The years went by; the laundry and shop were sold and the girls finished college and married. Jennifer became a mother as well as a teacher in North Carolina. Holly had a successful modeling career, married and became a mother. Byrd was remarried to Ed Krotine and lived in a beautiful Punta Gorda Isles home an area that had been a mangrove swamp when she came here as a young bride.

In today's hectic pace, one can almost look back with longing on the days when, instead of listening for the dial tone, you heard the friendly, "Number please."

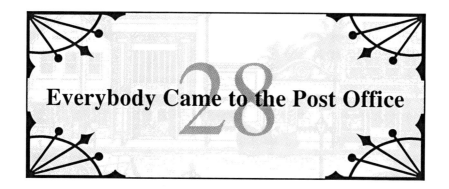

Everybody Came to the Post Office

The first mail delivery in this area came by schooner from Cedar Key, north of Tampa. When the railroad finally arrived, shipment by train was quicker and more expedient. The first post office (with the postmark of Trabue) was established in the year 1886 and it had a female postmaster, Nannie Scott!

Since that time, not only has the town's postmark been changed to Punta Gorda but the location of the post office has been moved from private home, stores and the Arcade to its present location on Marion Avenue.

Naturally, many local "boys" have worked for the post office. We've mentioned Joe Addison in an earlier chapter and, before his real estate and travel agency business, David Hill was the first rural mail carrier in Charlotte County in 1952. Victor Larrison, whose family dates back to the early settler, James Madison Lanier, had the first delivery route to Punta Gorda Isles, and one of our noted historians, U. S. Cleveland has poignant memories of his days at the post office.

We sure do take a lot of things for granted in Charlotte County. In spite of the fact that our population is booming, the system has been working pretty well. One of the things we take for granted is the post office. We look in our mail box and, generally, the mail is there. We go to the post office with our slip of paper and our package is ready. Considering where we've been, all that is a near miracle in a fast-growing area. It wasn't always thus.

When he started in 1938, U. S. Cleveland was a part-time postal worker. "There was the postmaster, two regular clerks and me. My job was to take care of everything that went on before 8:00 A.M. and after

6:00 P.M. Before the war, I worked holidays, weekends and vacations; always in the back, sorting mail or whatever. When I came back after the war, they put me on the general delivery window and I learned an important lesson.

"We didn't have any delivery services; everybody had to come to the post office to get their mail. We had only 911 boxes so there weren't enough to go around. Some families had to double up and a lot of people got their mail general delivery, especially those in the trailer park where there were about 500 families. Very often mail for the same family would be called for by three or four different members, each unaware the others had already picked it up!

"So I was looking for the same mail several times a day and the mail only arrived in the morning and at night after we closed. I was wasting a lot of time with people who had already been up to the window. To make matters worse, in the wintertime the mail would invariably be late, but the window still had to be open at 8:00 A.M. The mail wouldn't be ready, yet there I was waiting on people at the window and trying to sort and alphabetize the mail at the same time! The people kept *coming* and *coming* and I still couldn't make a dent in sorting the mail. I developed a phobia, I began to believe those people were coming over and over again to the window just to bug me. There'd be a line of them clear out to the sidewalk first thing in the morning. They'd come to the window and I'd say, 'I haven't got the mail sorted yet,' and they'd frown and zip down to the end of the line ready to pounce on me again in a few minutes. 'You get the mail sorted yet?' By the day's end I was worn to a frazzle; I was grouchy and ready to bite the head off anyone who looked at me cross-eyed. Then I realized I was letting the job get to me. I decided I wouldn't let those people get my goat; I'd let them think I was enjoying myself even if it killed me!

"One Saturday morning—Saturday was the toughest day because we closed at 1:00 P.M. and everyone else went home and left me to buck that line—I turned over a new leaf. I pasted on a big grin, asked them how things were going and got the mail out as fast as I could. Well, you know it was a funny thing, people were in a very good mood that day. Customers were smiling—it was a small miracle. Then I got to thinking that maybe my new attitude had something to do with their attitude; they were reflecting my mood. That was the beginning of a new theory of mine in dealing with the public; be nice to them and they'll be nice to you."

When Hugh "Mac" MacGibbon became postmaster in 1952, U. S. became assistant postmaster and he remarks, "When I got that job, I automatically became the complaint department and I really enjoyed taking a grouchy, snarling customer and sending him off with a smile. It was a challenge and I finally realized that I had come to the right conclusion for the wrong reason."

U. S. retired in 1974 but is always on the go, either showing the historical slide shows he and Vernon Peeples put together or supervising the public address systems for all types of civic functions. There is a lot of Will Rogers' homespun philosophy and humor in U. S. Cleveland. He is a delightful man and an interesting conversationalist. He is the ultimate resource for historical information in our area.

* * *

Victor Larrison was the first mail carrier to the newly developed Punta Gorda Isles and his problems were more with the weather than with people. He rode a regular bicycle (the three-wheel mailsters were to come later) and carried his lunch along with the mail in a big basket clamped over the handlebars. He was required to deliver mail only to the streets with 50 percent occupancy but he remembers pedaling down Palm Tree Drive to Dr. Ruchteschell's house which stood alone at the very end of the street.

He rode his bike in full uniform (no shorts in those days) and it got mighty hot during the summer. Many times he was soaked to the skin during the seasonal rainstorms. He'd have to get off his bike and push it through the downpour; visibility was so bad. But, in keeping with the United States Post Office tradition, Victor Larrison and the mail always got through.

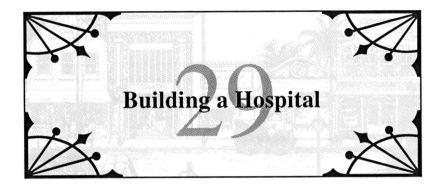

Building a Hospital

There was a time in Punta Gorda when the nearest hospital was miles away in Arcadia, a long trek for a severely ill person. A local physician, Dr. W. B. Clement, and some of his colleagues decided to do something about it. Edith Jones, niece of Sallie Jones (noted teacher for whom the Sallie Jones Elementary School is named) remembers Dr. Clement well. "He came to our house on Olympia seeking a donation for the medical center he hoped to build. People don't give him credit for all he did for the town. He started that hospital with very little money. After it was built, they discovered the building had termites. Dr. Clement put on old clothes, crawled under there and treated it because there was no money to have it done professionally."

Bernice Rountree, wife of Ebbie, the owner of the first Coca-Cola bottling plant here, said she watched with dismay while Dr. Clement used his skillful surgeon's hands to lay bricks for the foundation!

Ethel and Charlie Steele, owners of the Dutch Kitchen, had just recently moved to a large two-story house on Olympia. It had previously been owned by Dr. Alexander and was on the outskirts of town, surrounded by open fields and only a handful of neighboring houses. Suddenly the open fields were under excavation for the building of Punta Gorda's long-awaited hospital—Charlotte Hospital, later to be renamed Charlotte Community Hospital, Medical Center and then Charlotte Regional Medical Center. The old house stood as an oasis in the asphalt parking lot of the hospital.

When Cliff Daniels moved here from Cleveland, Ohio, in 1947, he had no idea how involved he was to become with the little town's growing pains.

Cliff had been a heating engineer in Ohio and had come here solely for his wife's health. He knew no one in the area and had no employment prospects. His first job was pumping gas at Jack Hindman's station on Marion Avenue and Route 41. Then he went to work for Dr. Clement who, aside from his medical practice, had a small marine-engineering business. "Doc had a beat-up dredge and one of my first jobs was to hydraulically lift the sand from the river bottom to build up the land where he planned to build his house on the river. We didn't need a permit to dredge in those days and there was no law then against removing a batch of pesky mangroves."

Charlotte Hospital had just been completed and, in its first months was running on a shoestring. December was a cold one in Florida that year. There was no central heating system in the hospital, just little floor heaters in the rooms. The patients' beds were piled high with blankets. Something had to be done and Dr. Clement thought of his new helper who had been a heating engineer in Ohio. The two men put their heads together and came up with an idea; the abandoned airfield on the edge of town had been handed over to the county and all kinds of equipment had been left there.

After getting permission from Vasco Peeples, who was chairman of the Charlotte County Board of Commissioners, Cliff went on a foraging expedition at the airfield. In the officers' quarters and the mess hall he found a treasure, coal-fired boilers.

"We got Slim Keys' wrecker, the only one in town (left over from a bomb disposal unit) and hoisted the boilers and radiation units. We converted the coal-fired steam boiler to a hot water system. The wartime Army had been able to procure anything, including coal from the north. The hospital couldn't afford that, so we changed to oil. The new medical center had a heating system at last!"

Faye Whitehurst (Mobley/Austin) had always wanted to be a nurse and, with the advent of World War II, she joined the Cadet Corps of Nurses. By the time of her graduation from the Corps, the war had ended and Faye was free to become a civilian nurse. The medical center had just opened and, after completing her boards in Atlanta, she began her nursing career at the new hospital in her hometown. Her stay at the medical center proved to be a lengthy one—forty years! She started first as a surgical nurse, then director of nurses and the last eleven years in the social work services department. She retired from her "home away from home" in 1987, able now to spend more time with her husband, Keith, and hopefully do some traveling.

* * *

Gussie Peeples Baker had known Faye for years, but not as a nurse, and their first encounter in the Medical Center had its wild moments. Always an irrepressible child, Gussie recalled the incident with an impish grin. "Dr. Clement had been trying to con me into having my tonsils out. He promised me, 'If you'll let me take them out, I'll do it the day the hospital opens its doors and you'll be the first patient.'"

"Doc" was true to his word and there is a plaque at the medical center with Gussie's name on it. She and her sister, who was the second patient, had the entire hospital and staff to themselves. Faye, the surgical nurse, had to chase the elusive Gussie (who had jumped off the operating table in a last-minute attempt to escape the operation) down the hall and drag her back to the operating room!

Nicknames are peculiar. Sam McCullough was always called "Mac," but his son, James, is always called "Sam." Figure that one out! Sam was born to Mac and Margaret McCullough in 1919 in a house where the courthouse later stood on the corner of Taylor and Olympia. He had Miss Norma Pepper for his first grade teacher as did so many other Punta Gorda children and graduated from Charlotte High School. He had a childhood sweetheart, Catherine Wilkins, and though World War II interrupted their courtship, the two were married while Sam was still in the service and Catherine was in nurses training at Tampa General.

After the war, the couple returned home to Punta Gorda and civilian life. When the medical center was completed, Catherine worked there intermittently as a surgical nurse. The couple by then had a daughter, Donna, and Catherine's first duty was at home.

Clara Hobson Rickards has been a hard worker all her life. Motherless at six, raised by her older siblings and father, she learned to pull her own weight early in life. At fourteen she became the lady of the house, taking care of her four brothers and father, doing the cleaning, cooking and laundry in addition to going to school.

After years of caring for her family it seemed only natural that Clara chose the nursing profession. After working for a doctor in Tampa, she returned to Shell Creek with her husband, Paul Rickards, to care for her ailing father. Upon her father's death, Paul too became sick and she nursed him through his last illness. Clara joined the hospital as a nurses aide shortly after its opening and "worked there for twenty years, although it seemed like only two." A woman who was truly dedicated to the caring of others.

There were many fine doctors in town at the inception of the Medical Center: Drs. Clement, Kline, Alexander, Shedd and Maxwell to name a few. Dr. Roscoe Steele Maxwell was the oldest son of Mary and Roscoe "Mack" Maxwell who owned Maxwell's Pharmacy. His parents brought him to Punta Gorda when he was only four. Perhaps it was his father's pharmaceutical background, but "Rocky" (as he was known to family and friends) always wanted to be a doctor. He went to the University of Alabama for premed, then on to St. Louis for part of his residency; Bay Pines, Florida for another portion and finally home to Punta Gorda, while finishing his medical education in Arcadia since there was no hospital here.

Rocky and his first wife, Janet, met while students at the university and were married in his parents' Punta Gorda home before he finished college. When he commenced his practice in Punta Gorda, he hung out his shingle on Olympia Avenue. His office was next door to the telephone company. He and Janet had two children, Lephia, and Douglas. When the hospital opened, Rocky became affiliated with it along with his regular practice.

Years later Rocky married Jane Beard, a registered nurse from Pennsylvania, and adopted her daughter. Then he and Jane proceeded to have two daughters, so Rocky was really surrounded by the fairer sex! The couple built a handsome home out on Shell Creek, complete with orange grove. The doctor led an overly busy life with his practice in town, the hospital and a full social calendar. His mother says that "Rocky could entertain a group of people for an entire evening and never repeat a word!"

One morning with his alarm set for six o'clock so that he could reach the hospital by seven, Rocky was found dead in his bed of a heart attack. The beloved Dr. "Rocky" Maxwell was sorely missed by one and all.

* * *

Emmett and Ruth Perkins (early pinery and Perkins Insurance Agency) became involved with the Charlotte Hospital from its very beginning. Emmett was one of the charter members of the hospital board and Ruth soon joined him there. She remembers the hospital as small (twelve beds) with only the bare essentials: emergency room, X-ray and laboratory.

In his years of canvassing for the hospital, Dr. Clement had met a wealthy Boca Grande lady who was impressed with the efforts of the townsfolk to support the small medical facility; she thought that a volunteer auxiliary would be a tremendous asset. Not only a woman of wealth, but of fierce determination, she recruited several ladies in the town who were active in community and church affairs. These included: Ruth Perkins and the Mmes. L. H. Caraher; L. V. Desguin; F. T. Gardner; E. Patterson; W. E. Guthrie and E. B. Yeager. One day in early March 1949 she invited the ladies to a luncheon at the big Hotel Charlotte Harbor. There was a lot of excitement in the air, luncheon at the beautiful old hotel was always a festive occasion. On this particular day, the chef outdid himself with a delicious meal and the ladies were equally inspired by their hostess to start the ball rolling for a volunteer auxiliary at the hospital.

Ruth Perkins reminisces, "The very next week we met at the Woman's Club and I remember Margaret Gardner, pen in hand, writing vigorously the first minutes of our organizational meeting." Mrs. Guthrie became the first president of the Auxiliary and Ruth Perkins was chosen to be secretary/treasurer. This was the start of the volunteer "Pink Ladies" of the Medical Center. Looking back, Ruth says, "In the beginning it was a struggle. We sent cards to everyone we knew asking them to come to a meeting, hoping to get additional volunteers. Our priorities at the start were to staff the little lobby desk and to plan events that would bring in money to buy things needed by the hospital. For instance, there weren't enough gowns for the patients, so we made them; I think I sewed three dozen. A local produce dealer offered us free watermelons; we wangled free ice from the ice house and advertised a watermelon party on the bayfront, fifty cents a slice. That's how we made money."

Ruth also remembers the first Easter at the hospital when someone on the staff approached her with the news that there weren't enough funds for a holiday dinner for the patients. "Emmett and I went out and bought the biggest turkey we could find. We took the bird to Clara Hobson Rickards, a nurses aide, and she cooked it at her home. The rest of us managed all the trimmings. Every patient enjoyed a delicious Easter dinner and no one ever knew how close we were to not having it."

Ruth and her husband worked and watched the little hospital and the infant auxiliary grow into a first-class medical institution. When the hospital's Wellness Center was started a plaque designated it the Ruth and Emmett Perkins Center for cardiopulmonary rehabilitation— a fitting memorial from Ruth to her beloved late husband.

When we look at the hospital today with its extensive remodeling and expansion, its up-to-date equipment and its full staff, it is heart-warming to remember that this all began with the determination and door-to-door canvassing of Dr. Clement and others. Also, let's not forget the ingenuity and hard work of Cliff Daniels and his scavenger hunt for boilers and other heating equipment at the abandoned Army airfield.

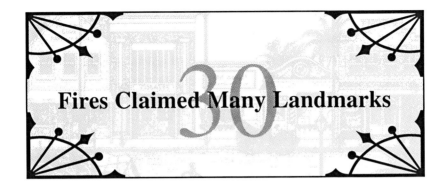

Fires Claimed Many Landmarks

One of the archenemies of people living in Florida at the turn of the century was fire. Dry timber, long dry periods of drought and sudden gusts of wind were a combination to feed many a blaze. James E. Whidden Sr., born in Charlotte Harbor in 1904, had two of his family homes destroyed by fire. The first one in 1906, he was too young to remember, but the second is still etched in his memory. While the fire raged, he and his father watched helplessly. "There was nothing at all we could do about it."

When Corrine Sias was growing up in the early 1900s, a trip from Harbor View where she was born in 1899, to Punta Gorda entailed a bumpy ride over a dirt road to the docks and then a one-mile boat ride to the opposite shore. Corinne remembers, as if it were yesterday, a big fire in 1910 when four houses in Harbor View were completely razed, her own home among them. There was no fire department, of course. The eleven-year-old girl was playing in her yard when she noticed the flames. The fire spread so quickly she never did manage to get inside to rescue anything. "No, land sakes, we didn't have any fire department; we just all helped pour buckets of water on it but we couldn't put it out."

The Hart family of Punta Gorda operated a large store on Retta Esplanade, which was completely demolished by a devastating fire. The building was not insured and the family returned to their native Philadelphia. Years later, Celia Hart returned on a visit and eventually married Edward Wotitzky (the parents of Leo and Frank).

Jacob Wotitzky, Edward's father, was one of the first merchants in our town and had a successful merchandise store on Marion Avenue west of Sullivan. Like the Hart family, fate in the form of a raging fire wiped out the business overnight. Again, there was no insurance.

Catastrophic fires were not unusual in old Punta Gorda. Most of the buildings downtown were one or two-story wooden structures, made of resin-soaked pine and highly flammable. There was no fire protection in those days and insurance premiums were prohibitive.

Punta Gorda lost many buildings in addition to the Hart and Wotitzky stores. The infamous fire of 1905 wiped out other businesses on the south side of Marion. Later, there were two pump trucks and a volunteer fire department. Nevertheless, the Taylor Street school went up in flames, the Princess Hotel and the movie house became embers.

Ira Atkinson, who was once our one-man police force in town, was also the first paid fireman. In 1924, the volunteer Punta Gorda Fire Department acquired a Seagrave fire engine and Ira was hired to drive it. He wasn't on the job long, however, when Joe DeWitt, chief of police, swore him in as the policeman of Punta Gorda! Eventually, Henry Koon became the one and only paid fireman; he and his wife lived over the fire hall at city hall and Henry drove the old Seagrave. Volunteers were the only help Henry had. It is rumored that some volunteers were paid "by the fire" and that fires increased during the Depression years.

It was the year 1948 and Cliff Daniels had been in Punta Gorda only one year when the town had one of its worst fires. The Texaco bulk gasoline plant on Nesbitt Street ignited and made a spectacular blaze. The whole town was lit up. At the time Punta Gorda had one fireman, Henry Koon, and of course, the volunteers. He roared the old Seagrave truck to the scene, pulled down the hose, unlocked the hydrant, turned the valve on and then ran like blazes to catch the nozzle, which by that time was writhing like a big fat snake. Finally our lone fireman was ready to pour water on the fire. When the drums in the warehouse caught, they exploded 100 feet into the air, spewing oil.

The volunteers and Cliff helped Henry all they could, but it was a total disaster. Only the overhead tanks were saved. Although a newcomer in town, Cliff had a long talk that day with Bert Sellen, superintendent of city works, and suggested to him that Punta Gorda sorely needed reorganization in the fire department and more volunteers.

Time passed and the reorganized and larger volunteer fire department was doing a good job. Henry Koon was still the lone fireman, but he had more help. Then somebody got the bright idea that the volunteers could use a little advertising with the public. They hit on the unique plan of displaying their skills to the townsfolk. They planned to stage a fire near Desguin's theater at an appropriate time. Vic agreed to cooperate.

As Cliff tells it, "There was a vacant lot where Hessler's carpet store is now. We dug two big holes there and filled them with trash, motor oil, tires and diesel fuel. We planned to light a huge fire just as the theater let out. Vic would call us the exact minute the movie was over; that was the cue to light the fire. We'd blow the whistle, rush down the street with the siren screaming, bell ringing and put out the fire while the entire movie house crowd watched."

Cliff and the other volunteers thoroughly planned this staged inferno. "We were going to hook up to the hydrant in front of the Seminole Pharmacy on Taylor and Marion. So, on the morning of the big day, we really tested that hydrant to see that it was flushed out and in good order. It worked just fine. We even thought to take the hydrant caps and nuts off and grease them, so they'd come off easily by hand."

But, as the poet said, "The best laid plans of mice and men gang oft agley." Bobbie Burns was right. Unaware of what the firemen were up to, an eagle-eyed and zealous water department employee saw the hydrant was dripping. He hopped out of his truck and tightened the nuts and caps securely with a wrench.

"That night when Vic called, we blew the fire whistle and took off down Marion Avenue under full siren." The theater crowd lined the sidewalk to gape at the blaze and speeding fire truck. The volunteers, enjoying their hero roles to the hilt, raced to the hydrant. Of course, they couldn't budge the securely tightened nuts! After many attempts, they finally sent someone back to the firehouse to get a heavy wrench, but by the time he returned with the tool, the fire was merely smoldering. To put it mildly, the crowd was not impressed!

The episode of the bogus blaze is amusing now to those who watched the fiasco years ago. They can now chuckle over the comedy of errors. It is amusing now to visualize poor Henry Koon rushing to secure the hose, unlock the hydrant, then rushing back to catch the nozzle while it squirmed in midair, but fires were no laughing matter in Punta Gorda. Businesses were lost, families were left homeless, lives were lost and old landmarks destroyed. One of the most dramatic and tragic of all the conflagrations was that of the great landmark, the big old hotel.

In August of 1959, Ike was in his second term as president, Hawaii, had become our fiftieth state. Punta Gorda was sixty-years old and its rambling hotel, now a health spa, was four years older. It was about two A.M. on August 14, and Homer Monson was tired. He had just finished working with his men, unloading fish at his family's Punta Gorda Fish Company. Having dropped the men off at their respective houses, he was on his way home when, in his words, "Along about the banyan tree on Retta Esplanade, things started to get real smoky. I got to Taylor Street, turned left up to the corner there—just past the hotel and saw fire glowing in the back part of it. It was quicker to drive to the fire station (now the Punta Gorda City Hall) than to get on the phone, so I turned and drove lickety-split down there."

Derrill Moore was the sole fireman on duty and, after setting off the siren, he and Homer drove pell-mell to the hotel—Homer in his truck and Derrill in one of the two fire engines. They pulled up in front of Larue Earnest's barber shop and dragged the hoses across the street. The siren still blaring, volunteer firemen were racing through the streets to fight the now roaring blaze. One of them, Cliff Daniels, dashed to the fire station and drove the remaining fire truck to the scene. In the midst of the confusion Willard Gandy, hotel caretaker, was rescued from the flames. He panicked, jumped into a nearby Dodge pickup, drove it through a hibiscus hedge, narrowly missing a bystander and ended up against the town water fountain!

Derrill Moore recalls, "The fire started in the central open stairway and elevator shaft. That's why it burned so rapidly." The wind was blowing toward Marion Avenue and frantic shopowners were trying to salvage what they could. Larue Earnest even had hauled his barbershop chairs out on the sidewalk ready to go.

Shirley Haas, a patient at Charlotte Community Hospital, remembers seeing the reflection of the flames dancing on her hospital room walls. She also recalls that her husband, Eugene, was not with her because he was down in the town helping Mr. Mobley, owner of the Seminole Pharmacy, rescue his cash register and pharmaceutical supplies.

Robert Barley recalls the night and all its excitement. He had come here in 1943, and married a local girl, Alice Brown. The couple, with their two children lived on the corner of McKenzie and McGregor. Robert was a volunteer fireman.

On that sultry night in August of 1959, Robert and his wife were awakened by the town siren and Robert "felt in his bones it was the old hotel," so he drove directly there. Crowds had already formed and "you could actually see the fire run from one end of a floor to the other, then hop to the next." Soon the place was an awesome inferno.

This had become a major disaster. Now the whole town was in danger, not merely the hotel. The Fort Myers and Arcadia Fire Departments had sent reinforcements. Suddenly the wind changed and blew towards the river and the bay. The town was saved, while the hotel burned on. Firebrands were glowing and spiraling into the bay; sparks and embers flew up and arced into the sky, landing as far away as the old fish houses; in modern terms—from Publix to Fishermen's Village.

The townsfolk flocked to the scene; most people throwing on bathrobes, jackets or coats over nightclothes. However, one eminent attorney, noted for his sense of propriety at all times, arrived at the site in a business suit, complete with shirt and tie.

The fire had now taken on the aspect of a beautiful spectacle, a glorious display of nature's fireworks, as spectators stood by in awe. Many had tears in their eyes, knowing that this marked the end of an era. The Grand Old Lady of Punta Gorda was no more.

Development Comes to "The Point"

It was the end of an era, but a new era had already begun. Belle Quednau's "crabbing grounds" and where Joe Addison used to race his pony on the sand flats west of town, were occasionally referred to by the townsfolk as "the point."

In 1956 when Frank Smoak Jr. was mayor of Punta Gorda, the city needed a sewage treatment plant and it was suggested that "the point" would be an excellent place for it. Frank's father, an ex-mayor, advised against it. "That point is going to be the future of this town. They'll dig canals and carve out beautiful homesites as they did in Biscayne Bay." As luck would have it, Charlotte County offered the old sewage treatment plant at the abandoned airfield and the "point" was spared.

Money had been allotted to dig drainage ditches for the mosquito control program which required an access road to accommodate a dredge and a pumping operation. The seventeen-acre area was named Ponce de Leon Park and it is difficult to imagine how unattractive a piece of property it was at that time. Most of the town fathers claimed it was "pouring money down a mudhole." Cliff Daniels, superintendent of public works, and in charge of the project, had his own misgivings.

A few months before Cliff had gone on a fishing expedition to the point. This meant wading through the mosquito-infested swampland, but the game and fish were worth it. "I was carrying my pole, a minnow bucket, and two or three snook I'd caught and was headed home when a little shoat scampered out of a palmetto patch, squealing and carrying on. The sow, a wild hog, saw me and thought I'd hurt her baby. That wild pig put down her head and charged. I hit her with the minnow pail and she charged again. This time I kicked her in the snout, losing my snook in the process. She finally quit and went back to her baby."

Cliff knew the lay of the land out on the point and the obstacles involved. The surveyors had to struggle through mud and mangroves to map out the course; a dragline had to be placed on mats to keep it from sinking into the muck. In spite of these precautions, the county bulldozer was mired for three days in the swamp before it could be winched out. Material that was dredged, sand and marl, was dumped to one side of the canal and furnished the necessary fill for the road. Later on this was spread, graded and compacted with bulldozers and roadgraders.

The surveying on this project was hampered by the dense undergrowth that climbed a tree. The surveyor couldn't follow the line with his eye. Finally, someone had a brilliant idea. A Piper Cub was flown in and, as the pilot hovered over the line, he would wave and "we would set the direction with an old ship's compass. We tore bedsheets and placed them as markers for the proposed direction of the line." Other obstacles were wire fences that had to be cut and then wired back when the men were through. Doc McQueen had some cows grazing there and he wasn't too happy about the road." Today, when we drive over the blacktop road to Ponce de Leon Park, we should be grateful to the hard-working men who pioneered the first access to the "point."

Gussie Peeples Baker remembers her first visit to the "point." Her dad, Vasco Peeples, took her on a jeep ride to "Fiddlers Flats," as the point was sometimes called. They bounced along the marshy land, looking at the vast expanse of muck and mire.

"The mosquitoes like to have hauled us right out of that jeep." Dad said, "We're going to build a road down here. We think the area is going to grow." I said, "Don't bother, you'll be wasting your time," and "Look at beautiful Punta Gorda Isles now."

In the mid-fifties the "point" where Cliff Daniels had locked horns with a wild pig, attracted the attention of some real estate developers who had made quite an impression in Fort Lauderdale, North Miami and Biscayne Bay. They were Bud Cole, Al Johns, Sam Burchers and Bob Barbee. Cliff recalls, "I took them out to the "point" in a jeep and

164

we still had to cut fences to get through that swampy land. Doc McQueen's cows were still there and I had to put the fences back up behind us, so they wouldn't get out. Doc wasn't happy about the development out there. He'd already had an invasion with the park project. He had leased all that area for pasture land."

After flying over "the point," driving on it, and scouting it from all angles, the young foursome decided "this was it" and on December 31, 1957 title to the first 550 acres of mangrove swamp passed to Punta Gorda Isles, Inc. Cliff remembers thinking, "Well, they'll build maybe a half dozen houses out there and it will be a nice addition to Punta Gorda."

The rest, as they say, is history!

Stick Frog and Candy Pulls

Of all our memories, those of our childhood are the sweetest. Here are some of our citizens' recollections of growing up in Punta Gorda.

Danette Dreggors: "Our house on Sullivan was surrounded by a pinery. At that time Virginia Avenue was only a dirt cart path. My friends and I planned our trips to the Seminole Pharmacy when Luster Mobley would be on duty, 'cause he served the biggest scoops of ice cream."

Benina Falany Huckaby Hancock: "I had lots of playmates and we made our own toys and our own fun. Our parents would join in the games, like hail over the house, stick frog, a form of mumblety-peg in which a knife was thrown into the ground. We would fan it, back it, fist it and elbow it. To win you had to put the baby in the branch, throwing the knife over your shoulder so it stuck in the ground. This was our favorite game. We also had peanut roasts, candy pulls, sing-alongs and later, dances. We had such fun growing up in this town!"

Sidney Parker: "There were weekly fishing expeditions up Prairie Creek and quail hunting with a slingshot. Johnny Jack had a sawmill near Charlotte High and we'd get a piece of tin roofing and slide down the sawdust pile. Hoop rolling was fun; we would form a wheel out of wire and, with a stick, propel it along the sidewalk. Once an automobile ended up in a ditch to avoid hitting my hoop-rolling brother."

Mary Agnes Crosland Fambrough: "I spent the first six years of my life at my grandfather Whitten's Pineapple Center. On rainy days little girls could find plenty to do in the big sprawling house and, when the sun was shining, we had the whole outdoors. Beside the pinery, there were cows and chickens. My father (T. C. Crosland) used to squeeze just enough milk from a cow to fill a tin cup and I would give that to my little kitten. I remember that the house was high off the ground to avoid flood water and the chickens hatched under the porch.

"Dad's boats (West Coast Fish Company) plied Charlotte Harbor stopping at the various fish stations along the way. The Indians would bring all sorts of things to these stations to barter for the white man's goods. Cap'n Fred Quednau had picked up three motherless bear cubs this way and carried them back to Punta Gorda. Daddy brought them home. They were cuddly and playful as could be when they were little. Dad built a large cage for them but let them run loose a good part of the time. Mr. Mobley of the Seminole Pharmacy had jokingly suggested that they might like some ice cream, so one afternoon Dad put the cubs on a long chain and marched them to the drugstore. A crowd collected and the bears put on a good act, standing on their hind legs, slurping up double-dip cones. The bears were very much a part of our family."

Edith Jones: "The town was very small, of course, old brick streets and really only two big avenues, Marion and Olympia. Mr. Alford let the kids swim in the hotel pool in the off season, and we had band practice in the community hall in the summer. My, it was hot! There were fans, but they didn't help much. Speaking of heat, one of my big joys at Christmas time was chocolate candy. We couldn't get much chocolate the rest of the year because it wouldn't keep. It was just too hot and the ice boxes were not that efficient."

Charlotte Steele Anderson and Jackie Steele Weeks: Our parents were very young when they married and probably because of this found time to have fun with us. They weren't much older than their offspring! We all went hunting for quail in the thick woods around town, went to Chadwick's Beach (Englewood) to fish and made trips to Warm Mineral Springs near Venice. When we went fishing, all we took was white bacon, black pepper, a loaf of bread, a sweet onion, some cracker meal, a hatchet (to cut the swamp cabbage), a pot to cook it in and a frying pan. When we got to Chadwick's Beach, Daddy would cast his net to catch bait for us. Then he'd leave us to do the fishing while he and Momma cut the swamp cabbage. Momma would clean the cabbage and start cooking it in the big pot while Daddy cleaned the fish we caught. Pretty soon we'd be sitting down to a feast of fried fish and swamp cabbage.

"We also loved the trip to Warm Mineral Springs. We'd all pile into Uncle Jim's Model T and off we'd go over the fields and through the woods. Uncle Jim knew where he was going and didn't follow roads. He'd head north through the fields until we got to the springs. We would park under a tree and all go swimming, coming out for lunch and then back into the water again. We'd spend the whole day there, just swimming and lazing. We loved it. Life was simple and families were close in the years preceding the war. No hustle, no bustle, just one day at a time."

Lonnie Friday Persons: "Those were fun days, school dances at the old hotel, swimming meets in the hotel pool, football and basketball games. The chef at the hotel prepared the most delicious food and the buffet was decorated with ice sculptures. Since Punta Gorda was small, everyone was welcome. It was a great place to grow up."

Gussie Peeples Baker: "Looking back on my childhood, it was fantastic. It makes me sad that my children couldn't have the childhood I had. Everybody stopped to help everybody and it was the time of neighborliness. At night people would sit on the corner of Marion Avenue and talk. We didn't have television. Then after visiting with friends, they'd go home and listen to their favorite radio program. Life was simple and nice."

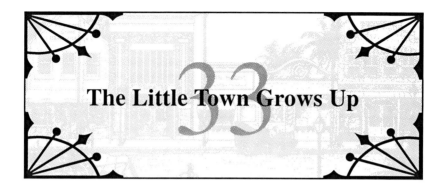

The Little Town Grows Up

The little fishing village and cattle town has grown up; the changes have been many. On Punta Gorda's ninety-ninth birthday, I wrote a column for the *Charlotte Sun* that still applies today. Here it is:

Last Sunday there was a love-in in Old Punta Gorda Park. To old-time Punta Gordans it must have brought back memories of long ago Saturday nights when everyone in Charlotte County came to town to visit, swap yarns, to shop and see the sights. Only this time there was music to add to the enjoyment, the unusual vista of a flotilla of boats, a hot-air balloon wafting in the sparkling sky, blessedly short speeches by dignitaries and the joyful singing of school children.

The day was perfect, the weather glorious and everyone seemed to get into the spirit of things. The brick street and the park that Ken Larkin had dreamed of three years ago provided an ideal setting for ladies strolling as in olden times in long skirts, high-button shoes, big hats and even gloves! Neighbor greeted neighbor, there were reunions of old friends, the band played in the gazebo. Food was plentiful and ran the gamut from newfangled hot dogs to old-time swamp cabbage, from "New Yawk" pretzels to grandma's cookies. There were laughing tots climbing on the old buckboard or splashing their hands in the old Hotel Punta Gorda fountain; kids riding ponies, strangers visiting with strangers, a feeling of fellowship and nostalgia.

If the late Vasco Peeples was watching, he would have been proud of the show his daughter, Gussie, had organized for the town's ninety-ninth birthday celebration. He would have enjoyed watching his son, Vernon, autographing his book about the town's history. It was a little different from Murry Hall's memories of the busy Saturday nights years ago. Nobody came on horseback or in wagons and there is a bridge now; if anyone came by boat, it was by choice, not necessity; but the same spirit prevailed as in the old days—a neighborliness we regained, if only for the day.

There were solemn moments, too, when a wreath was laid in the bay for the dead of Pearl Harbor and, as the band struck up "The Stars and Stripes Forever," our flag was slowly and respectfully raised from half-mast to its normal proud position. A moment of silence was respected by the large crowd. Then the band went on to lighter music and church choirs raised their voices in the approaching dusk. When the Sallie Jones school children finished their final chorus, the Christmas tree in Old Punta Gorda Park was lighted amid cheers.

Many of the people went from the Park to West Retta Esplanade to view the lovely vintage, turn-of-the century homes on the bayfront, sparkling with centennial lights. We drove silently, bumper to bumper, past the stately old homes decked out in their Christmas finery. Drivers slowed so others could join the motorcade; no impatient person blasted his horn as we proceeded at a snail's pace down the street. As we slowly passed the lighted homes, I could imagine clip-clopping at this leisurely pace in a horse-drawn carriage, enjoying the balmy evening breeze, to visit friends in a time when the latchstring was always out and the doors were never locked.

Changes come and changes go, but memories live on in this little town. Happy Birthday Punta Gorda! Merry Christmas and God bless!

About the Author

Angie Larkin began writing her column for the *Punta Gorda Herald*, which later became the *Charlotte Sun-Herald,* to promote the work of Old Punta Gorda, Inc. She and her husband, Ken, were active in the community and involved in preserving the town's history. Although she had no previous experience as a columnist, Angie Larkin discovered that people opened up to her and shared their stories about the

Angie and Ken Larkin

past. After writing columns for three years, she concentrated on putting her interviews into book form in time for the city of Punta Gorda's 1987 centennial celebration.

A native of Boston, she lived in Florida while attending art school. She and Ken were married for fifty-six years, had three sons, five grandsons, and one great-granddaughter.

.

Index

Bill's Bar, 98
Bill's Tackle Shop, 121
Bingley, Elizabeth, 144, 145
Biscayne Bay, 164
black community, 55, 89–92
Black Rock, 33
Blacklock, Bernice, 51, 152
Blacklock, Raymond, 51
Blossom Shop Florists, 88
Blount, B. B., 84, 91, 96, 97–98
Blount's Grocery Store, 71
Blountstown, Florida, 93
Boca Grande, 49, 50, 103
    Coles and, 73, 74, 75
    shipping, 95, 131
Boca Grande Pass, 31
Bokeelia, 72, 145
Bonnell, Annie, 143–44
Bonnell, Danette (Dreggors), 35, 36, 166
Bonnell, Omar, 143–44
Bonnell, Robert C., 143–44
Bonnell's Department Store, 144
Bowman, John, 113
Boyle, Sara, 39
Brabson, Margaret, 51, 96–97
Bradenton, 16, 49, 51
Bradentown (Bradenton), 16, 49
Breezeway Drive-In, 108
Brooksville, 130
Brown, Alice, 162
Brown, George, 89–90, 100
Brown, James, 54
Brown, Johnny, 66
Brown Machine Company, 54
Brown, Marijo (Kennedy), 26, 54
Brown's Dairy, 71, 96
Buckingham Air Force Base, 147
Burchers, Sam, 164
Burns, Bobbie, 160
Burnt Store Road, 86, 138
C
Cabbage Hammock, 59
Cahoun, Mr., 34
Calder, Lewis, 34
Caloosahatchee River, 19
Calusas, 1
Cape Coral, 141
Captain Allen's Rooming House, 144

Captiva, 2, 32
Captiva Pass, 33
Caraher, Mrs. L. H., 156
Carlos, 12
Carlos Pass, 33
Carmalita Street, 88, 147
cattle drives, 16–17, 19–21
cattle industry, 16–17, 19–21, 28–29
Cedar Key, 2, 119, 149
Centennial's Old Timers' Day, 72
Chadwick brothers, 30, 33
Chadwick's Beach, 51, 167
Charlotte Avenue, 55, 111
Charlotte Community Hospital, 152, 161–62
Charlotte County, 14, 22
    development of, 163–65
    education system of, 48–49, 54, 55
    Florida Legislature and, 47
    sheriffs of, 15, 114–18, 139
Charlotte County Administrative Offices, 26
Charlotte Drugstore, 71
Charlotte Harbor, 1, 2, 18–19, 24, 26, 45, 55, 65, 67, 91, 101, 108, 109
    alligator hunting, 22
    bridge linking Punta Gorda, 97, 104
    cattle drives, 16–17, 19–21
    drive-in theater, 108, 112
    fishing, 30–33
    postmaster of, 117
Charlotte Harbor Cemetery, 98
Charlotte Harbor School, 39, 40, 55–56, 127
Charlotte High School, 45, 46, 47, 50, 51, 52, 53, 55, 57, 58, 73, 88, 127, 140, 145, 166
Charlotte Hospital, 133, 152, 153, 156
Charlotte Regional Medical Center, 69, 152
Charlotte Sun, 169
Chokoloskee, 33, 48
churches, 49, 54, 88, 92, 100. *See also specific churches*
Churchill, Winston, 5
citrus groves, 34, 68, 73, 95, 129–30
Clement, W. B., 99, 152–57
Cleveland, 89, 90, 100, 102, 144
Cleveland, Andrew, 144

Whidden, James Edward Sr., 18, 24
Whidden, Jimmy, 24
Whidden, Joanne, 24
Whidden, Josephine (Taylor), 24
Whidden, R. E., 17
Whidden, R. J., 22
Whidden, Robert J., 18, 24–25
Whidden, Snake, 18–19, 22, 24–25
Whiteaker, Jean, 72, 130–32
Whiteaker, Nora, 130
Whiteaker, U. S., 54, 75, 130
Whitehorse, Faye, 85
Whitehorse, Jeanette, 85
Whitehurst, "Doc", 80, 107, 123
Whitehurst, Elsie, 68, 123, 133
Whitehurst, Faye (Mobley-Austin), 68,
     107, 132–33, 153–54
Whitehurst, "Little Doc", 107, 123–25
Whitehurst, Percy, 123
Whitten, William Monson, 53, 57
Whitten's Pineapple Center, 166
Wilkins, Catherine, 154
Williams, Bertha Mae, 14, 56–57
Williams Stock Company, 104
Willis, Alma (Howland), 101
Willis, Carl, 67
Willis, Charles, 145
Willis, Claude, 101
Willis, Jim, 145
Willis, Mary (Dampier), 145
Willis, Mott, 30, 67–68
Williston, Florida, 10
Wilt, Gladys (Roberts), 16, 49
Windmill Village, 82
Winn-Dixie, 74
Winter Garden Ornamental Nursery, 138
Woodville, 135
Wotitzky brothers, 42
Wotitzky, Celia (Hart), 46, 65, 158
Wotitzky, Edward, 46, 65, 70–71, 158
Wotitzky, Frank, 41, 47, 65
Wotitzky, Jacob, 46, 65, 158–59
Wotitzky, Laura, 70
Wotitzky, Leo, 41, 43, 44, 46–47, 65,
     81, 105, 107
Wotitzky, Zena, 47
Y
Yeager, Areta, 87, 112, 134

Yeager, E. B., 134
Yeager, Ed, 134
Yeager, Mrs. E. B., 156

CPSIA information can be obtained at www.ICGtesting.com
Printed in the USA
BVOW04s1236151214

379143BV00003B/516/P